# Golf's Best Excuses

**JOSHUA SHIFRIN**

**FOREWORD BY GARY PLAYER**

Skyhorse Publishing

Skyhorse Publishing books may be purchased in bulk at special discounts for sales promotion, corporate gifts, fund-raising, or educational purposes. Special editions can also be created to specifications. For details, contact the Special Sales Department, Skyhorse Publishing, 307 West 36th Street, 11th Floor, New York, NY 10018 or info@skyhorsepublishing.com.

Skyhorse® and Skyhorse Publishing® are registered trademarks of Skyhorse Publishing, Inc.®, a Delaware corporation.

Visit our website at www.skyhorsepublishing.com.

10 9 8 7 6 5 4 3 2

Library of Congress Cataloging-in-Publication Data is available on file.

Interior illustrations by Ian Baker.

Cover design by Tom Lau
Cover illustration credit Ian Baker

ISBN: 978-1-5107-4475-2
Ebook ISBN: 978-1-5107-4476-9

Printed in China

For Maya, Gilad, and Idan.  I love you!

# Table of Contents

# Foreword
## by Gary Player

The harder you practice, the luckier you get. Golf is a puzzle without an answer. I cannot fix a hook that you slice. These are just a few of my favorite quips when I joke around with friends and clients alike on the course.

Indeed, golf is not for the faint of heart. It's a game that a child can master, but an adult can find extremely difficult even with an entire lifetime of practice. The possibilities for such a passion are plentiful and can lead to joy or internal agony.

The passion for golf manifests differently in each individual. You need not be a devoted athlete. Although, in my case, athleticism has helped me play this game for more than seventy years. So, because I have played thousands of rounds with professionals and amateurs, it comes as no surprise that I have heard thousands of excuses. Maybe more than anyone who has ever played this game. It's not a game of inches, but millimeters. You might get quite a shock when you realize that being off by just a fraction can cause your ball to hook or slice.

The margin of error is what separates golf from other sports. How amazing is it that we as players try to accomplish the seemingly impossible task of making a tiny ball go into a little hole from hundreds of yards away? I am still trying to figure out the best way to play the game. But the important thing is to have a passion and to make sure it's one without time limitations attached to it.

The excuses we make are just that: excuses. You know you can do better. And as an avid golfer, you certainly have practiced enough to be a scratch player, right? Not so fast. It was not until I turned seventy that the secret to the swing I learned from Ben Hogan truly made sense. So it is quite comical to think about the excuses I made when I hit a bad shot, especially when I first discovered the game. I simply didn't know how to swing properly for the majority of my life! Now, you may beg to differ when you think about the eighteen Major Championships on the Regular and Senior Tour I won. I feel it could have been twice as many if I'd fully understood the golf swing like Hogan did.

Even with the trials and tribulations of attempting to perfect your swing, golf rewards you with the healthful side effects of long walks, fresh air, and, sometimes, good company.

Ask yourself the question, *Why do I play golf?* An enthusiastic player will find every excuse in the book to get out on the links and have some fun.

But the game of golf provides us with a never-ending stream of challenges to our honor and dignity. My point here is that golf is, of course, only a game. But it is a game that loves you back. Even with all the excuses, I know of no man, woman, or child who ever felt that the game somehow let them down.

So no more excuses; just enjoy this great game.

*Black Knight Archives*

# Introduction

I love golf! I love everything about it. From the anticipation of my weekend round, to a pint or two in the nineteenth hole, and everything in between. I love the scenic beauty, the feeling of stepping into the tee box of the first hole on a crisp, clear morning. Gripping and ripping a driver on a long par five. Watching a long putt with a huge break creep up and gently drop into the hole . . . it's just paradise. There is truly nothing I would rather do than spend a few hours on a beautiful course with a few of my best comrades tackling one of sports' greatest challenges. And when all goes according to plan, and I walk off the eighteenth green with a score in the 70s, it's a feeling of total eureka!

But what happens when the unthinkable occurs? You've got it all figured out. Just keep your left arm straight. Keep your head still on the putt. Widen your stance just a bit. These small changes in your game will surely lead to the best round of your life. And then it all falls apart. You start to hook your drives like a Saturday night call girl. Your irons are leaving divots in the fairway that resemble the potholes in New York City. You couldn't sink a three-foot putt if your life depended on it.

It doesn't matter if you're a Grand Slam champion or a weekend hacker. It won't help even if you're a scratch golfer or the most athletic of your friends. Eventually, this great game that we all love so much, dream about at night, crave when we're at work, and can't get enough of when we're playing well, will inevitably take your "A" game and turn it to rubbish. This most sensuous of paramours will grab you by the throat, shake you like a baby with a rattle, and tear your heart out. And the worst part about it is your game always seems to fully fall apart just when we think we have it mastered. How bitterly cruel.

So what is one to do? Like any true addict in the throes of one's dependence, admitting that he or she has a problem, or even worse, making the decision to quit, is simply out of the question.

Well, despair no longer. In *Golf's Best Excuses*, you can explain away your pitiful play. With these hilarious, tried and true excuses, you can let anyone who will listen know why your seemingly miserable performance isn't actually due to your ineptitude as a golfer, but instead a mere result of forces that are truly out of your control.

So if you're having a bad day and you've hit your third

straight shot into a hazard, or put that snowman onto your scorecard, feel free to use one, or more, of the multitude of excuses in this book to restore order to your world of chaos.

So I say to you, dear friend, the next time your game goes straight down the tubes, don't despair. Simply turn to *Golf's Best Excuses,* and you'll laugh your way right back to one of the most worthwhile of endeavors . . . another round of golf!

# Best Professional Excuses

When I was just a young pup with a small set of plastic golf clubs and big dreams of stardom, my parents used to tell me, "If you want to be the best, you need to learn from the best." Thus, I guess it goes without saying that if you're looking for some tried and true golf excuses, a good place to start would be with the professionals. So without further ado, here are some of my favorites from the PGA:

"I made the putt. It just didn't go in."
> —Tom Kite explaining why his putt narrowly missed its intended destination on the final hole at the Masters.

"I don't want to make excuses, but I did have cancer."
> —Paul Azinger was noted for using this excuse in a humorous fashion after successfully defeating lymphoma.

And what is one to do if your justification doesn't fully make its point? You can always follow the great Tiger Woods's example by simply repeating the same excuse over and over again. Not sure what I mean . . . well, take a look at the following:

"Again, I left a lot of putts short out there. The greens were a little bit slow and I tried to put some more hit in my stroke, but putts were dying off the front of the lip."
—Tiger Woods at the 2012 British Open

"I just couldn't believe how slow these greens were . . . They're slower than the (practice) putting green . . . struggled getting the balls to the hole."
—Tiger Woods at the 2012 PGA

"I just thought the greens were so slow. Yesterday they were so quick and dried out and today they were so much slower. From the first eight holes I think I left every putt short. I had a hard time getting the speed and being committed to hitting the putts that hard."
—Tiger Woods at the 2013 Masters

"I struggled with the speed all week. These greens are grainy. It's one of the older bent grasses, creeping bent. So it's a little bit grainy. I struggled with the speed, especially right around the hole."

—Tiger Woods at the 2013 US Open

"I had a hard time adjusting to the speeds. They (the greens) were much slower, much softer. I don't think I got too many putts to the hole today."

—Tiger Woods at the 2013 British Open

That's right, in five straight majors Tiger explained his futility by blaming the speed of the greens. I say that if it can work for one of the greatest golfers of all time, it can surely work for you and me.

# Excuses for the Rest of Us

If you weren't duly inspired by the best our sport has to offer, why not try one or more of these excuses on for size . . . it just might do the trick.

### "I thought that was a six iron, not a nine."

This is a perfect excuse to use the next time your shot comes up short of its mark. But you're going to need to sell it. The first thing you're going to want to do is to start rubbing your eyes. You may want to let your compatriots know that you just lost a contact lens. Complain about seeing spots and your depth perception. And if that doesn't work, and you're getting desperate, try letting anyone who will listen know that your ophthalmologist has been on an extended vacation and you simply reversed the numbers. And of course you'll want to finish up by stating, "I really hit that one flush, I can't believe I confused my clubs again."

### *"The grips on my clubs are worn."*

If you want this excuse to work, you might have to go to an extreme . . . but be careful, or someone could get seriously hurt. You're slicing your drive like a master butcher with a beautiful piece of meat. You can't hit your irons, and you're putting like it's your first time on a green. You're on the back nine, and there is no salvaging your round. Look for the perfect opportunity when no one is in the way, line up your tee shot, take a big backswing, and let your club fly about 50 yards down the fairway. That will surely get everyone's attention. Then spring it on them . . . "I had a feeling that was going to happen. I've barely been able to hold on to my clubs all round. I really need to get them re-gripped."

### *"I thought this cross-handed putting grip would have helped."*

You've surely heard of the classic quip about how to score in golf: "Drive for show, putt for dough." Slamming a big drive off the tee gets lots of oohs and aahs, but that 250-yard

monster doesn't count any more than a one-foot putt. And when it comes to actual scoring, the challenge of stroking that 1.68-inch-wide ball into a 4.25-inch hole has driven many a hacker to distraction. There are several approaches to improving your putting, including endlessly shopping for the perfect putter; looking at the hole, not the ball; working on tempo; using a croquet stroke (illegal), mental health counseling; and changing your grip. So in desperation, you have gone to a cross-handed grip in which your left hand is lower than your right (assuming you're right-handed). You've tried it with great success on a practice green, and now you're being tested by a simple three-footer on the eighteenth hole, with the match on the line. While your opponents are watching, make sure to tell them this is the first time you've used this new grip. (I won't tell if you've been using it for weeks). You apply the cross-handed grip, line up the putt, adjust your stance, take a calming breath, and execute a super smooth stroke . . . I won't keep you in suspense. You blow it. Your ball ends up sitting on the edge of the hole, your subsequent tap-in costs you another full stroke, and there goes the match. So what do you do now? Simple. Hang your head like countless thousands of other golfers have done, curse under your breath, and mutter, "Damn! Same old, same old. I was sure my new cross-handed grip would have made a difference this time."

## *"These greens are faster/slower than normal."*

Your putting is atrocious. You three- and four-putt on a regular basis. You've got little to no feeling in your hands, and the notion of "touch" on the green is like Greek to you. Not to worry. The next time your putt doesn't end up anywhere near the hole, take a few practice swings. Then use your acting skills from your high school play to good use and put a knowing look on your face. And if you really want to push it, take a long practice putt and then look at your watch as if timing the velocity. Then try telling your fellow golfers, "The speeds on these greens are completely different than what I'm used to. I'm normally a terrific putter."

## *"I've got a bad back."*

This excuse is pure gold because many golfers have legitimate back problems. And every golfer knows that if your back is bothering you, it's almost impossible to play well. However, to use this excuse to its fullest, start showing *symptoms* early in your round. Groan loudly when you pick up your tee. Get down on one knee when you bend down to pick up your ball.

Make sure to engage in stretching exercises whenever anyone is watching. And at the end of the round try uttering, "I guess it's true what they say, it really kills your game when you've got a bad back."

## "I didn't spend enough time on the driving range before my round."

As we all know, practice makes perfect. So the next time your game starts to go astray, take a few extra rehearsal swings before each shot. Make sure it's perfectly clear that you didn't have the time to get to the course early, and consequently didn't have your usual warmup session on the range. And also specify that just like any exceptional athlete, without the proper pregame ritual, it's hard to play your best. You might want to finish with, "I just can't groove my swing like normal. I really wish I was able to spend more time on the range this morning."

## "The course just didn't play well."

Because, of course, you are a terrific golfer (ah-hem), you deserve the best. The best equipment, the best treatment, and surely the course should be groomed to perfection. Therefore, the next time you record your third straight double-bogey, why not blame the course? I mean, the top professional courses use the best groundkeepers, and yours clearly should as well. A player of your caliber deserves nothing less. So when the inevitable occurs, and you hit a ball out of bounds, take a long time to look at the divot. You might even want to pull out a few blades of grass and start to mumble under your breath about the poor quality of the sod. And then state loudly, "I don't want to cause any trouble, but they really need to talk to the grounds crew; this course played terribly today."

### "There were too many spike marks on the green."

*Drive for show, putt for dough.* Any golfer worth their weight has surely heard this expression. Even if you can consistently drive it 300 yards, without a good short game, you're just not going to score well. And if you end up three-putting several times throughout your round, make sure to get down nice and low, maybe even on your hands and knees, and examine the green closely. If someone actually has the audacity to walk across your through line, make sure to huff and puff. Then try this one on for size, "This is why I need to play earlier in the morning. All of those spike marks on the green completely threw off my putting."

### *"My golf clubs are too old."*

We all know the golfer who is always trying to buy oneself a better game. By purchasing a new piece of equipment, one is sure to improve their game. And the best part about this excuse is we've all been there. With a flashy new driver, or a belly-length putter, we are sure that will make the difference. In reality, the only *difference* is usually found in our pocketbook, not our scorecard. So when you mishit your third shot in a row, hold up your club, examine it closely, and start to mumble about the poor construction. State loudly that these clubs are as old as dirt. And then utter the following, "My equipment is completely outdated . . . I really need new clubs."

### *"I'm all juiced up today, and I'm hitting the ball farther than normal."*

This excuse is definitely a winner because clearly the reason

you're playing poorly is because you're actually too good of a golfer—gotta love that! If your round has gone down the drain anyway, the next time you're within 50 yards of the hole, try pulling out a 5-iron. Grip it and rip it well past the hole, then quickly put your club back in your bag before anyone can catch you red-handed. Then try this one on for size . . . "I did it again. I hit my wedge 170. I normally only hit my wedge about 150, but all of my recent weight-lifting has clearly added length to my game."

### Did You Know?
At the 1945 Los Angeles Open, Babe Zaharias became the only female golfer to date to make a cut on the PGA Tour when she shot a 76 and 81 in the first two rounds respectively.

### "The birds chirped during my backswing."
This one's a no-brainer, although you'll have to lie with a straight face. You have just flubbed a shot. Doesn't matter

how, whether you topped it, shanked it, whatever. Just throw up your arms in frustration and demand a Mulligan because there was a loud bird chirping during your backswing that started halfway through your downswing. And when you're playing partners refuse to give you a free shot . . . "Hey, I'm not Tiger Woods. How'd you expect me to stop my swing right in the middle?"

### *"I've been so busy at work that I haven't had time to practice."*

You've been looking forward to your Saturday game all week. It's a beautiful day, and you have spousal approval to play a full eighteen holes and then hang around with your buddies at the 19th hole. What could be better? But it becomes quickly apparent that you haven't brought your "A" game. By the third hole, you're already five over par, and your confidence is farther away than the ball you have just hit out of bounds. You have to come up with a viable excuse, and quickly. While no one is looking, program your smartphone to ring after another hole or two, then have a fake conversation with someone who's calling you about work (yes, on a Saturday!). Then grump to your playing partners: "Can you believe this? I just put in a 60-hour work week, and they're bothering me on a weekend. How can I play well when I've had no time to go to the range?" Then shake your head in disgust. "I just can't put in so much time at work and still play a decent game of golf."

### "I'm late for my wedding, and it's throwing off my concentration."

This one will test how big a lie you're willing to tell, and whether you're capable of telling an even bigger lie to negate the first one. (Bear with me . . .) You're in a club tournament and are scheduled for a match with a guy you barely know. You've heard he's been playing well recently and you need an excuse in case you lose. For this one, you have to plant the seed even before you tee off. Arrange for an early tee time, and when you arrive, tell the guy you're getting married later that day. When he expresses surprise, explain that you had to do a lot of fast talking to get your fiancée's approval to play, but you're concerned that she was not happy about it. But you're not getting married. You're not even engaged, but he doesn't need to know that. And if the match is going badly, purposely hit a couple of balls into the woods and take your time about finding them. If you're artful enough, your round will start to go overtime. That's when you begin to look at your watch and furrow your brow. Purposely scull a shot or two and mutter about the time. Now you're off the hook. The match won't count if you simply throw up your hands and say, "Listen, I'm sorry, but I'm going to be late for the wedding, and I just can't concentrate."

*(PS: You may be wondering about what happens when the guy next sees you and asks about your new marriage. That's when you have to step up and say your fiancée was so angry about your playing golf that day she called off the wedding. If you can do this, read no further. I bow to a master of prevarication. As George Costanza of* Seinfeld *fame once said, "It's not a lie if you believe it.")*

## "I thought this hole was a dogleg to the left . . . not right."

Let's face it. When you stand over your driver, or a long iron, you may be aiming right down the middle of the fairway, but in reality, you have no idea where your shot will end up. Not to worry! The next time you hook your drive, or slice your three iron on a dogleg, and your shot goes in completely the wrong direction, start by shouting out, "I'm the man!" And when your compatriots look confused, you can follow that up with, "Wait just a gosh-darn minute. I meant to hit that fade/draw. I had no idea the dogleg went in the opposite direction."

### *"My golf instructor completely screwed up my game."*

As any good parental figure will tell you, "Practice makes perfect." And sometimes a couple of lessons with the club pro is all that you need to improve your play. But what happens when those little tidbits of gold actually end up causing your game to take a couple of steps back? The next time your round is going into the toilet, I suggest you start mumbling to yourself about how your pro has filled your head with nonsense. And make sure to speak just loudly enough for your playing partners to hear you utter something to the effect of, "Did that clown tell me to stand closer to the ball, or further away?" Eventually, when you need to break out your calculator to add up your round, make sure to tell anyone who will listen, "If it weren't for those stupid lessons, I surely would have broken 80 like I normally do . . . I want my money back."

### *"The wind keeps shifting directions."*

Ok . . . so the reality of the situation is that you haven't been on the green in regulation since the Reagan administration.

You're over the green, short, left, right, and you haven't taken a long walk with your putter in so long that you basically can't remember what the club even looks like anymore. But alas, I've got the perfect excuse for you. The next time you miss the green, or hit one out of bounds, bend over and pull a few blades of grass out of the ground and let them flow in the breeze. Or you may want to pull out the tried and true act of sticking a finger in your mouth and holding it in the air. And when you have everyone's attention, let them know that, "The wind keeps shifting directions. My kingdom for a good weatherman!"

## "I was hitting them great on the range."

As any athlete will tell you, pressure can be a killer. Sure, some of us thrive when the heat is on. But if you're like me, and you have a three-footer on the 18th hole for a 79, the word "yips" doesn't even begin to do it justice. So the next time you're chewing up the course like a puppy with a pair of your favorite shoes, just start to mumble to yourself. Let your playing partners know how well you were hitting them in the solitude of your early morning warm-up. We've all been there, and clearly this excuse will gain you some sympathy. A one-liner of, "I don't know how I could be such a disaster when I was hitting them so well on the range" will likely be followed with an affirmative head nod or two.

### *"I need more lessons."*

Oh, to be independently wealthy. Wouldn't it be great if we didn't have to worry about money, and could simply think about our golf game? I don't know about you, but one of the first things I'm planning on doing once I win the lottery is to hire my own personal golf instructor. But alas, until those six lucky numbers come up roses, I'm stuck as a self-taught hack. Yet sometimes you can use your poverty-level income in your favor. When you're on the course, ask your foursome for some tips. Let them know that you hate to keep pestering them with questions, but you simply can't afford to hire a professional. And when you're on the 19th hole, finish the day with, "If I only could afford more lessons, I'm sure I'd be on the tour by now."

### *"Your cigar smoke keeps getting in my eyes."*

There are a lot of reasons why so many people love the great game of golf. The great outdoors, the comradery with your

friends, or that high like no other . . . a perfectly struck shot. And for as long as golfers have been teeing it up, there are players who just love to fire up a stogie as they play their respective rounds. However, if tobacco isn't your forte, but your buddies just can't get enough, why not use it to your advantage? The next time you duff a shot like Homer Simpson at Moe's Tavern, try to work up a hacking cough. Then make sure to rub your eyes incessantly. And of course follow all of that up by telling your chimney of a friend, "Your cigar smoke keeps getting in my eyes. How can I be expected to play under these conditions?"

## *"I was looking at the wrong green."*

We've all done it. From the pros to the weekend hacker. Every golfer, at one point or another, hits a ball so far off-target that it's hard to imagine where they were aiming in the first place. And of course, some of us are more prone to errant play than others. But not to worry. If you're anticipating hitting a few wayward shots, my advice is to use the old tried and true poor sense of direction excuse. To start, you might want to show up about five minutes late for your round. Let your foursome know that you got lost, yet again, getting to the course. You can then laugh at yourself as you tell your compatriots that you can't find your way out of a paper bag. And finally, when the inevitable happens, and your ball doesn't land in the same ZIP code from the intended target, just pretend to stifle a smirk and say, "My darn sense of direction, I was actually aiming for the wrong hole."

## Did You Know?

*Mike Austin recorded the longest drive ever in professional play when he hit a 515-yard bomb off the tee at the Winterwood Golf Course in Las Vegas, Nevada in 1974. Incredibly, the mammoth shot landed 65 yards past the flag on the par-4 fifth hole.*

### "These clubs are new, and I'm not used to them."

If you are like many of the golfers I know, you'll do anything to improve your game. From lessons, to instructional books, to extra time at the range, most golfers spend a lifetime looking for the silver bullet to lowering their handicap.

And although there are countless ways to approach this most worthy of endeavors, none seems as easy as simply "buying" yourself a better game. If I had a new putter, that would do the trick. Golf shoes with longer spikes are surely the answer. But alas, as we all know, throwing a few dollars at your game will only take you so far. So the next time you find yourself with more snowmen on your card than you'd find at the North Pole, make sure to mutter under your breath about the feel of your clubs. Take a few extra swings as if you're trying to get used to the new weapons. And finally, when the massacre is over, just tell anyone who will listen that, "I just got these new clubs and I'm simply not used to them yet."

### *"I keep picking up my head."*

We've all done it. You say it to yourself five times right before your shot. "Just keep my left arm straight. Make a good turn. Hit down on the ball." Only to do the exact opposite when we're striking the ball. And one of my personal pet peeves is picking up my head too quickly. If this often happens to you as well, there is a good excuse . . . but it takes a little bit of acting. Start by doing a little bit of twitching. You may even want to blink your eyes repetitively and start to mumble about those SOB's who are after you. Then, the next time you duff your shot, tell 'em, "I just can't seem to keep my head down. I really need to get back to my psychologist."

## *"My opponent lied about his handicap."*

This excuse is appropriate for the big time. Sure, you want to play well every time you go out for a round, but when you're in a club tournament, the pressure is really on. And if it's a handicap format, this excuse just might do the trick. Say you're down three holes after the front nine. Start to mumble about how well your opponent is playing. You don't want to speak too loudly, or the guy might just whack you with his four-iron. But if you lose after playing your heart out, go to the 19th hole and drown your sorrows in a frosty beer. Then tell the bartender, "That guy won, but he's a cheater. He said he had a 27 handicap, *same as mine*, but even though I shot a 74, he beat me by two strokes!"

## *"I shouldn't have gone right for the flag."*

If you're anything like me, there's no better feeling than a long walk with a putter in your hand. But let's be honest for a minute, if my ball ends up anywhere in the vicinity of the pin I'm normally ecstatic. And because I generally have no idea where my ball is headed, I generally just hit my shot in the neighborhood of the hole, say a couple of Hail Mary's, and let the carnage ensue. However, if you have some real chutzpah, you might want to try this one on for size. Start to complain about the weather conditions—it's too windy, too humid, etc. Then, the next time you hit one about 50 yards past the pin, try the following: "I normally can leave my approach shots within ten feet of the hole. However, with these terrible conditions I really shouldn't have gone right for the flag."

### *"If I didn't have those four double bogeys I could have scored really well today."*

When I was a child, my father used to tell me a joke about a man who claimed that he only needed another $995,000 and he could be a millionaire. If you find that at all amusing this excuse might be right for you. First, make sure to tell your playing partners that you're having a really off day. You've never played this badly and you have no idea why your game has fallen apart . . . perhaps you did something horrific in a past life and the golf gods are now getting even with you. Then, when you're adding up all the chalk, you can explain it with, "Even though I had a horrendous day, if it weren't for the front nine, and those other six holes on the back nine, I could've scored really well."

### *"You should have given me that putt."*

We've all been there. Standing over a three-foot putt with a case of the yips. And I hate to tell the younger readers of this book, but it only gets worse with age. If this scenario describes you, there is something you can do about it, especially if you're not in tournament play. First, make sure to be very generous in giving your partners any possible putt. You can say something like, "Sure, I realize that's a 12-footer with a huge break, but that would be a gimme for me, so I'll let you have it as well." Then, the next time you miss your sure thing just say, "I always make putts of that length. It really threw me off when I wasn't given a gimme on that one."

### *"Someone yelled 'Fore' during my backswing."*

The professionals hate when this happens, so why can't it apply to us weekend hackers as well? No one needs to know that you regularly shank, slice, and hook three out of every four drives. And it will be our secret that you consistently take divots the size of New York City potholes out of the fairway. To set this up, make sure to tell the other golfers that your game is so precise, that any distraction can throw off your perfectly balanced swing. Then, make sure to let everyone know that you have exquisite hearing. And finally, when the inevitable happens, and your game goes to hell, just tell 'em, "Don't tell me you didn't hear that jerk yelling 'Fore' from six holes away? It completely threw off my impeccable timing."

### *"I can't seem to judge the distance of these new balls."*

I've been playing golf for years, and to be honest, I still feel like I have no idea what the hell I'm doing most of the time. Consequently, if my shots end up anywhere in the vicinity of where I'm aiming, well, I'm one happy camper. So to properly implement this excuse, you'll need to let your playing partners know on the first tee that this isn't your usual brand of ball. Sure that doesn't matter a lick . . . but I won't tell. Then, the next time your effort lands about 50 yards from the pin, of course you can explain it by saying, "I just can't seem to get a good feel for these new balls."

## *"My ball had a scuff mark on it."*

I know, I know . . . half the time it doesn't seem like it would matter if you were playing with a golf ball, a basketball, or a beach ball. Yet we still all make sure we try to benefit from every little advantage we can get. We use every ball washer, clean off our clubs, and even pick the grass out of our cleats. So the next time your shot goes awry, explain it as follows: "I just realized my ball had a scuff mark, which surely explains my three triple bogeys during this round."

## *"Sweat got in my eyes."*

I ask you, dear reader, is there anything better than going out for a round on a beautiful summer day? However, as we all know, with a summer day comes the heat. To properly set up this excuse, the first thing you want to do is lose your hat. Then, if you're not sweating enough naturally, you can always pour a little water on your head. Make sure to rub your eyes continually, and when you miss your next three-foot putt, or shank your drive for the fourth time on the back nine, just tell your friends, "I just can't see the ball properly with all of this sweat in my eyes."

---

### Did You Know?

*There are approximately 125,000 golf balls that end up in the drink surrounding the island green at the TPC Sawgrass's 17th hole.*

---

## *"Your shadow distracted me."*

Golf is a difficult game . . . and that's putting it mildly. Many of us play for years only to continually have this cruel paramour leave us feeling totally inferior. To play at an even somewhat respectable level, it takes one's absolute concentration. Consequently, when a player is addressing his or her shot, as we all know there is no talking, no movement, nothing that could cause even the smallest of focusing difficulties. So if your game is falling apart, make sure to complain about the player 50 feet from you who was moving during your putt. Then, the next time you misplay your effort, let your partner know that, "Your shadow is very distracting. It completely threw off my concentration." (And if it's a cloudy day . . . well . . . maybe don't use this one?)

### *"I forgot my sunglasses."*

Most likely, if you're reading this book, you're a lover of the great game of golf. Personally, there are few things that I like more than spending a few hours smacking around that little white, dimpled ball. And it doesn't matter if it's raining, a cool fall day, or windy. It's always a thrill. But nothing is better than playing on a crystal-clear, sunny day . . . unless, of course, your game has gone off the rails. In this case—if your eyes can handle it—try ditching the sunglasses. Squint as much as you can and let your friends know that you can't believe how stupid you were to leave your sunglasses at home. And if, by chance, someone offers you an extra pair, thank them for their offer, but politely let them know that the same contours of your face that make you extremely attractive, also, unfortunately, require custom-made sunglasses. And at the end of any horrific round, simply say, "I surely would have played up to my normal scratch game if only I had remembered my sunglasses."

## *"I've never had a lesson. . . I'm self-taught."*

You didn't play golf as a kid, and when you started watching on TV with the pros performing on those idyllic, landscaped courses, you decided to get in on the action and take up the game yourself. How difficult could it be with all that modern equipment? You just take a swing, and the ball soars like an eagle to the putting green. Meanwhile, you're enjoying a pleasant walk in a parklike setting, followed by camaraderie over a frosty mug of beer in the 19th hole.

What could be better? A slam dunk, right? But then you visit the local driving range, and it doesn't go exactly as planned. Still, you stick with it until you realize it's hopeless and finally admit to yourself that you need lessons. The problem is that you've bragged to your friends that you're a natural athlete and that they're wasting their money on golf instruction. So you decide to do it on the sly. You sign up with a pro in another town and don't say a word to anyone about it. The pro teaches you the fundamentals, and after three or four lessons your heart soars when he casually remarks that you might have already reached the potential of playing bogey golf. So now you're on the course for the first time and are playing with borrowed clubs. You're full of confidence, even though you're wearing cutoff jeans and sneakers. When it comes time to give out the handicaps, your buddies take one look at you and laugh. And just for a little added insurance, you remind them once again that you're self-taught and this is your first round, so they give you two strokes per hole. Your selective memory about your pro's comment makes you think you are now a bogey golfer, so when they set up a bet for ten dollars a side, you keep a straight face and tell them you're in. It doesn't take long for reality to set in. You manage to hit a number of decent drives and fairway shots, but a few blowup holes plus the elements of course management and the short game do you in. When it's all over and you've scored somewhere north of 120, you have to acknowledge the game is harder than you thought. But keep your head high and forget about integrity: "Okay, it's not that easy, but I've never had a lesson. If I'd spent a thousand hours with a pro like you guys have done, I'd be kicking your butts!"

### *"My ball was sitting in a divot."*

As we all know, golf is a game that requires tremendous skill. However, Lady Luck often plays a role as well. When you slice that ball into the trees, or hook it onto the golf path, only to see it take a fortuitous bounce and end up on the fairway, it can change the whole trajectory of your round. But

what happens when the golf gods work against you? If your iron game has deserted you and you've completely lost confidence in your mid-range game, when no one is around, stand over your ball and sigh heavily. Get down on your hands and knees and stare at the ball for an inordinate amount of time. Then take a swat at the ball. And if your iron play holds true to form, and the turf ends up going further than your ball, just follow that up with, "If it weren't for bad luck, I'd have no luck at all. This is the third time this round that my ball has ended up in a divot."

### *"I'm just not keeping my left arm straight."*

It always mystifies me that I can tell myself to do something 20 times, and then do the exact opposite. "Stay down on the ball," "Make a good turn," "Keep your head still, damn it!" And yet somehow I do the exact opposite. Now this one may be a bit of a stretch, but if you really want to sell it you'll have to break out your acting skills. Tell your friends that you've recently banged your head and your short-term memory has been temporarily impaired. Then, the next time your shot goes to hell, just say, "I just can't remember to keep my left arm straight no matter how hard I try . . . this damn short-term memory of mine!"

## *"My caddy was terrible."*

Surely your ineptitude as a golfer can't be all your fault. You've been playing for years, been practicing, and taken countless lessons. Plus, you were the third-string right fielder on the Junior Varsity baseball team in high school, so clearly you're not completely devoid of athletic talent. So what's the remedy? If you can afford it (after all, what's the cost of saving face?), then go with a caddy. Make sure to ask your caddy lots of questions. "Which way does the putt break?" "Is this hole a dog-leg left or right?" "What's the yardage to the hole?" And of course, make sure that all of your playing partners can hear you. And then, after the carnage, just let everyone know, "My caddy was awful! How can I expect to break 70 with such poor advice?"

## *"The group behind us is rushing me."*

I often hear my friends talk about how they like to play a quick round. Yet I just don't get it. I love golf, and I want to take my time playing. Not to mention the fact that the skill and precision needed to execute at the top level clearly takes patience. So the next time your game falls apart, you can always blame the frenetic pace. It doesn't matter if the group behind you is a single player, or a bunch of ninety-year-olds. Make sure to keep looking over your shoulder. Complain that you were nearly hit by a shot from the group behind you . . . it doesn't matter that it was a good 75 yards from you. And at the end of the round, you can tell anyone who will listen, "How am I expected to play at my best when I had to rush through my round? Tiger Woods surely wouldn't put up with this. Why should I?"

### *"This distance on this sprinkler head is clearly wrong."*

Ok, so you've never been very good at math. You forgot how to do long division the day you graduated, and you've never looked back. But now you can use this to your advantage. To set this up, even if you are playing well at the time, make sure to question the distances on the sprinkler heads overtly. You might want to ask, "Can the measurement be right? I normally hit my pitching wedge 170, but this sprinkler head said it's 180 and my shot ended up pin-high." And keep that one in your back pocket. The next time your approach ends up way off the mark, just come back with, "I hit that shot flush. I knew these sprinkler heads were wrong."

## "The sand in these bunkers is like hitting off of concrete."

Have you ever noticed how good the professionals are at getting out of the traps? They make it look so darn easy! Just aim a little behind the ball and carve up a little sand with your shot . . . no problem. I mean I do it half the time on the fairway, so it shouldn't be that difficult. Yet somehow it is. If you're in a precarious sand situation, before you hit your shot, you need to set it up. Like any good boy scout will tell you, be prepared. Mention how dried up the sand looks. Loudly state that it looks like the traps haven't been watered in weeks. Then, when the inevitable happens, and it takes three or four swats to get off the beach, just say, "I'm normally terrific in the sand, but these bunkers are hard as a rock."

## "The course was so crowded that the slow pace threw off my game."

So let's say you're playing with your usual Saturday foursome, and to keep it interesting, maybe there's a small wager on the outcome. Your playing style is about keeping a rhythm and moving right along, but this round is going excruciatingly slowly. You rack up a couple of double bogeys, and before long it becomes apparent that your cash is about to fly right out of your wallet. So what to do? You may subscribe to the notion that golf is a gentleman's game, but here's a tip, buddy. Forget it! Being a good sport might look good on TV, but show me a good loser and I'll show you a loser! Before your game goes completely down the tubes, start to squirm and whine about the slow play. Keep grousing while looking at your watch. Make a pretend phone call and let your playing partners overhear that your wife is raggin' because you're going to be late. Slam your clubs back into the bag after you've topped the ball or chunked a shot. And if you want to milk it all the way, completely forget about conducting yourself with any kind of class. Just hand over your two bucks and walk off the course after about the twelfth hole. Finally, don't forget to leave a parting shot: "This was crap! How can I play decent golf when it takes five hours to finish a round!" (You might lose your friends, but what the hell, it's more important to save face, right?)

### Did You Know?

*A hole-in-one on a par-five is informally known as a "Condor." This incredible feat has only been verified four times in the history of the sport to date.*

## *"I hit it off the heel/toe of my club."*

Obviously, you're good-looking, successful, a terrific ath-lete, and an even better golfer. Need proof? Just look at your Facebook profile . . . it says it all right there in black and white. So, if you're not playing well, there's got to be a good explanation. After the first few poor shots, let your playing partners know that you just feel a little bit off. You've never played this poorly, and it's just so hard to explain why. Then, the next time you shank a shot, rationalize it with, "That one went off the heel/toe of my club. I'm just a little off today. I'm actually worried that I might not break 80."

## *"I forgot to take my allergy medicine."*

One of my favorite things about the great game of golf is getting to spend a few hours on a beautiful, scenic course. Nature can be beautiful and at times awe-inspiring. However, the great outdoors can also have a negative side, and one difficult element for many of us is dealing with allergies. But aha . . . I say why not use this to your advan-tage. If your game starts to fall apart, I suggest starting with a little cough. If things get worse, begin to rub your eyes. And after your fourth triple bogey, break out into a full sneezing attack. Then, when your round is over, undoubtedly everyone will sympathize when you say, "My gosh darn allergies were just horrendous today. They truly got the best of me. I really wish I had remembered to take my allergy medicine."

### *"My knee hurts from an old football injury."*

So, let's say you stand about 5 foot 6 and tip the scales at 140. Not the biggest guy in the world, but you've been playing golf since you were a kid and enjoy bringing the big guys down to size with your finesse on the links. Plus, you've been on a roll lately so you can't resist some trash talking. "So whaddya think, guys, maybe I'll play left-handed today." Or, "Sorry fellas, I can't give you more than two strokes a hole." And the best part is that during the front nine you back it up. You're so far ahead that you start to lay it on thick. "Anyone want to make a side bet? C'mon, I'll give you odds. How about ten to one on a dollar?" Now your buddies have had enough. They all take you up on it, and you look forward to adding insult to injury. You crack a long drive off the 10th tee and snicker when you see their shoulders sag.

But on the 12th fairway, an old adage sets in. *"Pride goeth before the fall."* You shank an easy pitching wedge into a sand trap, then catch the ball cleanly without taking any sand and send it into the next fairway. A shocker, but no biggy. Just one hole, an aberration. Still, a stab of doubt enters your thoughts. At this point, you can start to plan for a possible downfall. Start to limp mildly between shots. Then, periodically grab your knee. And before you know it, if you blow up completely, ultimately leading to the humiliation of having to fork over three 10-dollar bills, you'll have your built-in excuse. Now the tables have turned. On the 19th hole they give it back to you in spades, and they're not about to let up. For a moment you panic, but not to be deterred you go to the bottom of the barrel. Staying calm, you lean back, take a casual swig of your beer, and say, "Just so you guys know, on that twelfth hole I tweaked my knee from an old football injury." This leads to a lot of hooting and hollering. "Right, a football injury! If a guy your size ever got tackled, you'd disintegrate!" And of course you have never set foot on the gridiron, but you're ready with your comeback. "Oh yeah? Did you ever hear of a field goal kicker? Normally there's no physical contact, but my knee injury happened when a defenseman ran into me while my leg was extended." And who knows? If you can keep a straight face, they might actually buy it!

### *"I continually second-guess myself . . . I should really go with my first instinct."*

We've all done it. From a test in school to picking a meal at a restaurant. We all second-guess ourselves. But this can work to your advantage if you need a good excuse on the course. Make sure to let your compatriots know that you're having a tough time making up your mind. I should go with the six iron, right? Or maybe the seven? That putt looks like it breaks left . . . or maybe right? Then, the next time you blow a shot, just try getting out of Dodge by saying, "If I had just done with my first instinct that shot would have been perfect. Why do I keep second-guessing myself?!"

### *"I forgot my sand wedge."*

As I've mentioned previously, one of the most difficult parts of a round is to get out of the traps consistently. If this is a problem for you as well, you'll need to set it up early in the round. Make sure to let your compadres know that before the round, you spent some time in the practice bunker and were hitting 'em like a pro. Then, during the round, if you find yourself on the beach, tell your friends, "Oh no, I left my sand wedge in the practice trap. Clearly, if I had it, I could put the ball a couple of feet from the pin. I guess I'll just have to do my best with my nine iron."

### *"I teed my ball up too high/low."*

Even for the professionals, getting off of the tee can be one of the most difficult parts of a round. There are just so many little things that can go wrong which lead to monumental problems. But surely it can't be your swing that's the culprit. Before you get up to tee off, let your friends know that you've been contemplating a new tee height. Although your driver is normally your best shot, and you regularly go 275 off of the tee, you are just trying to get a little more distance. Then, when your drive dribbles away, just follow it up with, "That drive would have been fine if I just didn't tee it up too high/low."

### *"I didn't think I could hit that club so far."*

I've played a lot of different sports in my life, but few athletic

endeavors have brought me as much joy as gripping and ripping a long drive or iron right down the middle of a beautiful fairway. Yet if you're anything like me, you're not always sure where that little magical sphere is going to end up. If this sounds like you, there's a way to get out of Dodge the next time your shot misses its target. First, do a couple of push-ups right before your round. Then, make sure to put on a tight shirt so that your bulging muscles are really displayed to their maximum benefit. Then, the next time you hit a flyer that goes about 30 yards past the green you can explain it with, "I've got to stop pumping so much iron. I had no idea I could hit that club so far."

### *"I keep forgetting to follow through."*

Similar to keeping your head down and keeping your left arm straight, many golfers often forget to follow through on their swings properly. Sure, we remind ourselves constantly, but in the moment, it's easier said than done. If your follow through leaves something to be desired, make sure to tell your group that you've got a lot on your mind. Work has been hectic, and your kids are driving you crazy. Then, the next time you push a ball out of bounds, make sure to say,

"With my mind so cluttered, I just can't seem to remember to follow through."

## "I usually play on nicer courses."

As I've previously mentioned, one of my favorite things about the great game of golf is the scenic beauty. I love a glorious walk through 18 holes of sheer splendid nature. And asking me to pick my favorite golf course is similar to picking my favorite child . . . I just can't do it. But that doesn't stop me from using it as an excuse. The next time you put a snowman on your card, start to complain about the speeds of the greens. Then you might want to mention that several traps weren't raked properly, and it seems as if the fairways haven't been mowed in days. Then, when your round is over, stick your nose up in the air and say, "I just can't play well on a mediocre course."

## "That was a perfect swing . . . clearly the golf gods have it in for me."

As we all know, to play the great game of golf well it takes a great amount of skill, practice, and talent. But sometimes it takes a little bit of luck as well. We've all hooked a ball into the woods only to have it fortuitously hit a tree and bounce out onto the fairway. And we've also all seen the other side of the coin where a perfect putt rims out of the cup. So the next time you're chalking up the high scores, just follow it up with, "I put a perfect swing on that ball. The golf gods are definitely against me today."

### Did You Know?

On February 6, 1967, golf was played on the moon when Alan Bartlett "Al" Shepard, Jr. hit a one-handed six iron in outer space.

### "I didn't want to hit the group in front of us."

Sure . . . you generally hit your drives 300 yards—*wink, wink.* You've let all of your friends know what a big hitter you are. But now you're getting ready to play with your foursome and, as they say, "the rubber is about to hit the road." Make sure to start by complaining about how crowded the course is. You might even want to vent about the "senior citizens" in the group ahead of you. Then, when you hit an 80-yard drive off of the tee, you've got the perfect cover. Just hit them with, "I could have bombed that drive like I normally do, but I wanted to make sure I didn't hit it into the group in front of us."

### *"I misread the break."*

Putting is maybe the most fickle part of golf. We've all had the experience of having a favorite putter fail us, then try another one that works for a while, and sooner or later reverting back to the original one and finding that it feels great in your hands. But the truth is, it's not the club, it's the guy who's using it. Or as it's been said, "It's not the putter, it's the puttee" . . . (although I freely admit I don't know if "puttee" is the right word here, or if it's a word at all). Anyway, you know what I mean. So what can you do when your putting stroke fails you? Well, you can always criticize the greens—too fast, too slow, etc. Personally, I like to gripe that the contours of the green are misleading. But you need to establish this excuse well in advance. In the middle of the round, make a comment like, "There's something fishy about these greens. Have you guys noticed that the ball doesn't take the break the way it's supposed to?" And when the big test comes and you blow the all-important putt, you have set the stage for your pronouncement. "Would you look at that? There's definitely something wrong with these greens. I misread the break because that ball actually turned uphill!

## *"I usually don't play with this type of golf ball."*

Clearly, you're a golf aficionado, and you love the game. You read about the sport, watch it on television, and play whenever you get the chance. And although you may not be ready for the professional tour, you're clearly prepared. You've got a nice set of clubs and a new golf outfit, so you definitely look the part. Unfortunately, your game doesn't always follow suit. But not to worry. At the beginning of the round, let everyone know that you're playing with a new ball. Then, at the end of the round, when you fail to break triple digits, just say, "I just couldn't get used to this new ball. Clearly, if I had stuck with the old tried-and-true, I would have scored in the 70s per usual."

### *"It's amazing how poorly I've been playing since I broke 70."*

We've all heard that in sports one of the hardest things to do is to repeat a great performance. Whether that's a professional championship, or simply a good round of golf, we've all been there. Make sure to tell everyone you know how great you played a couple of rounds ago when you scored in the 60s. Then, when you shoot a 95, just explain it with, "I don't know what's going on? Ever since I shot under par, my game has gone to pieces."

### *"I think the shaft on my putter has a slight kink in it."*

Drive for show, putt for dough. We've all been there. A great drive off of the tee, followed by a great iron to the center of the green only to end up with a three putt. For this excuse, make sure to tell everyone how much you love your putter. You've been using it for years, and it has clearly served you well. You almost never three putt with your favorite weapon. But recently, your putter seems to have let you down. Then it won't be a surprise to your group when you four putt two holes in a row. Just say, "Clearly there is

something wrong with my putter. I'm guessing the shaft has a slight kink in it. There is no other way to explain my woeful putting."

## *"I usually carry three wedges."*

As most astute golfers know, during competition you're limited to fourteen clubs in your bag. That's more than enough for most of us to get through our round. But if you're a little more particular, you might want to try this one on for size. The next time you're playing in a competition, and are restricted by the 14-club rule, be sure to tell everyone in the clubhouse before the round what a burden this is on your game. Then, when you lose 7 and 6, just tell your competitor, "I normally carry three wedges, and it completely threw off my game. My congratulations nonetheless."

## *"I never felt comfortable over the ball."*

Some days we have it, some days we don't. We've all had that feeling while getting ready to strike a golf ball, fleeting as it may be, that we're just going to hit a perfect shot. But more often than not, many golfers stand over their ball just praying that things won't completely fall apart. If this sounds like you—or even if it doesn't—let your fellow golfers know that you normally have a single-digit handicap, but recently you've been struggling. Surely they'll understand. We've all been there. Then, when you shoot a 97, explain it with, "I don't understand what's happened to my normally tight game. I just can't get comfortable over the ball."

### "The ball washer was awful."

Anyone who has a little OCD will definitely appreciate this excuse. Most of us know that a ball in flight, or rolling on the green, is a precise operation. Any little bit of wind—or worse, speck of dirt on the ball—can change the trajectory of the ball just enough to throw off your shot. To set this up, spend an inordinate amount of time at the ball washer. Make sure to inspect your ball, then wash it again. Do this several times while sighing deeply and loudly. Then, after the next blunder, try uttering, "The ball washer was awful. I just couldn't get the ball clean, and it wholly ruined my shot."

## *"My golf glove shrunk in the dryer, and now it's too tight."*

It goes without saying that because you are an exceptional golfer, you require the best equipment. And if everything isn't just right, it can throw off the fine-tuning necessary for an expert like you to play at your best. After your third double bogey, start to tug at your glove. Flex you glove hand in a grandiose manner that draws attention. Then, when the round is over, blame your significant other. "I can't believe I let my better half do the laundry again. He/she has clearly shrunk my golf glove again."

## *"I always put it in the water when I use a new ball."*

Yes, I know, you're a terrible golfer . . . don't worry, I won't tell. You couldn't hit a ball toward its intended target if your life depended on it. But isn't it just incredible that if there is an area you're trying to avoid, the ball always seems to go straight toward it? So the next time you're hitting over water, be sure to let your group know that you're using a new ball. Then, when the inevitable occurs, and the ball goes right into the drink, just say, "I knew that ball was going to go into the hazard. It happens every time I use a new ball." You'll surely get some head nods with knowing sympathy.

**Did You Know?**

Golf was invented in Scotland over **500** years ago. And incredibly, it is believed that the Chinese developed a similar game all the way back in **943 AD**.

### "I usually play much better."

As every statistician will tell you, if you gamble enough eventually the odds will catch up with you. But if I had a nickel for every gambler that came out of the casinos saying "I win more than Iose," let's just say I would have a lot more money to blow on roulette. The same motto seems to hold true on the golf course. So the next time you're struggling through a round, start to mutter about how poorly you're playing. You just can't understand what's happening. You're playing well above your handicap, and the only thing that makes sense is that you've clearly upset the golf gods. Then, when the painful round ends once again, just hit them with, "I don't know what happened today. I usually play so much better."

### *"My perfect shot hit a sprinkler head, and it ended up out of bounds."*

Golf is truly a game that requires tremendous skill to perform at the highest level. But like any worthy endeavor, a little luck never hurts as well. But what happens when the golf gods are against you? We've all been there. Hence . . . this is a great excuse. Make sure to let your group know how well you've been hitting your driver and long irons. You've been hitting them long and straight. There's just no stopping you. Then, the next time you hit way off the mark, just say, "Did you see that? I ripped another one right down Broad Street, but it obviously hit a sprinkler head and ended up out of bounds."

### *"The cigar I was smoking during my round made me sick."*

Even if you've sworn off tobacco of all kinds, consider storing a big smelly cigar in your bag in case you need a way to weasel your way out of a bad round. You can use it to stink up the air so badly that it will throw off your opponents. And if they don't like it, that's their problem. Courtesy is for players who just want to play a pleasant round of golf and aren't all that worried about winning or losing. So let's assume the foul-smelling smoke will distract your opponents, but will it improve your play? No, it won't. So if you're well into the round and you sense that you're going to lose, fire up that stinky stogy, take a big puff, and then go into a loud coughing spasm. Lay it on thick, even force yourself to gag a little. When the other guys express concern, wave them off. But go through the same thing a few minutes later, and then throw that disgusting, soggy thing on the ground and stamp on it until it's pulverized. I think you know where I'm going with this. When it comes time to criticize each other's game at the 19th hole, you're ready with your excuse: "I'm gonna have to rethink my brand of cigars. That one I was smoking today made me so sick I couldn't see straight."

### *"I'm hitting the ball so cleanly today that it's going further than usual."*

This excuse is one of my personal favorites. If your round starts to go awry, try letting everyone who will listen know how well you're playing. Then, the next time you miss the green by 50 yards, reiterate that you're on fire. When your fellow golfers ask what in the world you're talking about, just let them know that, "Sure, I'm not scoring well. But I'm just hitting the ball so cleanly that it's simply flying off the club. I don't know about you, but I'd rather play this way then like you, even though you're outscoring me by 10 shots."

### *"I couldn't wear my lucky shirt because it has a stain on it."*

If Ricky Fowler is known for his fluorescent golf outfits, and Tiger always wears black and red when he's in the Sunday hunt, why can't you have lucky apparel as well? If your game is going off the rails, the first thing you need to do is let everyone know that your washing machine is on the fritz. Not only is it inconvenient—and expensive to fix—but to make matters even worse, you couldn't wash your lucky shirt. Then, when the round is over, and your scorecard reads triple digits, hit them with, "How could I expect to play well when I couldn't wear my lucky shirt because it has a stain on it?!"

### *"I just had a lesson, and I'm not used to my new swing."*

As the saying goes, take two steps forward, one step back. This statement can be quite true when you're trying to improve any aspect of your life—especially your golf game. So if your game ends up deserting you, let the foursome know that you've just come back from a lesson with the pro. You received some terrific tips, but the professional warned you that it's going to take a while to really incorporate them into your game. However, because you're a go-getter, you've decided to use these new suggestions on day one right on the course. Then, when you end up with the "L" on your forehead at the end of the round, not to worry. Try saying, "Clearly I'm not used to my new swing yet. But in a couple of weeks, I'll be wiping you all up with my improved game."

### *"I was supposed to meet my wife an hour ago. . . we'd better play the back nine quickly."*

As we all know, golf takes impeccable precision and complete concentration to perform at one's best. It, therefore, goes without saying that if you're rushed, it can throw you off your game. So if your game is falling apart at the turn, and you don't see it coming back on the back nine, set it up as follows. Continually look at your watch. Pick up your cell phone and have a make-believe conversation that you're moving as fast as you can. Then, tell your partner you're in a huge rush. After the unavoidable back nine collapse occurs, rush to your car but just take one parting shot by saying, "I'm an hour late to meet my wife. How can she expect me to play well when I'm always being rushed?"

### *"I feel weak from hunger."*

This one is a no brainer. Everyone knows that it's hard to do anything well when you're hungry . . . let alone play a round of golf. So if you start to play poorly, start by complaining about how weak you feel. Then mention how loud your stomach is grumbling. And if you happen to see the food cart drive by, make sure to mention that the junk they serve doesn't go with your new healthy lifestyle. And finally, after you tally up your miserable round, just explain it with a simple question: "How can I be expected to play well when I'm starving?"

## "That was a perfect swing . . . I just picked the wrong club."

Golf is obviously a very difficult game. But with the weather elements, slope of the hole, pin placement, etc., it can be doubly harrowing. The professionals have an expert caddy with them to help with distance to the hole, but normally we weekend hackers are on our own. The next time you have a difficult shot, mutter loudly to yourself how you're in between clubs. Then, if your shot misses its mark, you can easily follow it up with, "I struck that ball beautifully . . . I simply picked the wrong club."

## "I usually take a cart."

Because golf can be played at any age, most golfers assume that you don't have to be an athlete, or in shape to play the game. Though this may be true to some degree, if you've ever walked 18 holes carrying your bag, you know it can be a good workout. The next time your group insists on walking, let them know that you're game, but that you'd really rather take a cart. Yet because you're such a good person, you're willing to take one for the team. Then, at the end of the round, if you end up in the precarious situation of having to buy the drinks, do so graciously. But of course add, "Good round gents, but that was exhausting. I would have been much better if I had taken a cart."

> ## Did You Know?
> Most golf balls have between **300** to **500** dimples; **336** dimples is a common number on many golf balls.

## "You were moving while I was in my backswing."

Because golf is a game of precision, any little distraction can lead to a poor shot. That's why the rules of golf etiquette require silence and a lack of movement when one of the players is addressing the ball. And of course, if necessary, you can use these unwritten rules to your benefit. The next time you're scoring poorly, make sure to start your swing but stop it abruptly before you make contact with the ball. Then look around and sigh loudly. Try doing this several times throughout the round. Then, when you really hit a whopper of a bad shot, come back with, "I just can't focus when people are moving during my backswing."

### *"The greenskeeper's mower was distracting me."*

As I've mentioned several times, golf requires immense concentration. Even the most minute loss of focus can turn a spectacular shot into a disaster. So why not use this to your advantage? First, let your partners know that you have excellent hearing, so please keep the volume to a minimum while you're hitting. Then, if your game goes down the tubes, just complain about all of the noise from the mower. If your friends tell you that they didn't hear any such noise, just come back with, "Like I told you, I have phenomenal hearing. There was definitely a mower several holes away, and it threw off my entire round."

### *"I always play poorly when there's a crowd watching me."*

It's called performance anxiety, and we've all fallen victim to it at one point or another. Whether it was during a test in school or asking out a significant other, we've all been there. So when you step up to the first tee, or come up to the 18th hole in front of the clubhouse, make sure to let your group know that you've always struggled with anxiety. You've actually been in therapy for years, but it hasn't helped much. Then, when you whiff on your shot, just say, "That would have never happened if I was out for a round by myself. But I always play poorly when people are watching me."

### *"I didn't keep my head down."*

It's one of the cardinal rules for playing well. We've been told repeatedly from the first day we picked up a club to keep our heads down. Then why is it so hard to remember? The good news is it's a built-in excuse that your friends will surely buy, as we've all been there. Make sure to complain early on that you've got a lot on your mind. Your kids have been driving you crazy, you've been fighting with your significant other, you've had a lot of pressure at work—anything will suffice. Then, when you flub your next shot, try uttering, "I've just got so much on my mind, I can't seem to remember to keep my darn head down."

### *"All of this early morning dew caused my putt to end up short of the hole."*

There's nothing like waking up early to play a round of golf. I've often wondered why it's so hard to get out of bed early on a work day, but how I can pop out of bed before my alarm to play a round of early golf on a clear, crisp morning. And if you're struggling to find your putting stroke, you can use this to your advantage as well. Start by complaining about the speed of the greens. They're just so slow today, and you can't seem to get your ball to the hole. Then, after you've three-putted for the fourth or fifth time, you can say, "Aha! I just figured it out. All of this early morning dew on the greens has completely thrown off my normally impeccable putting."

### *"I should have pulled out/left in the pin."*

To leave in the pin or to take it out? If you're just off of the green, it's a question we all struggle with. I know it's a rarity, but just in case, if you find yourself in just such a predicament, make sure to express your consternation. Then, if your ball rims out with no flag, or bounces off of the pin with the flag in, you'll have the perfect excuse: "I knew I should have pulled the pin/left the pin in. Why do I always seem to make the wrong decision?"

## *"I forgot there was a bunker there."*

It doesn't matter if you've played this course a hundred times in the past. If you're playing a blind shot, before you hit make sure to tell everyone how poor your memory is. If your head wasn't attached, you'd surely forget it. Then, if your shot goes astray and ends up on the beach, you'll have a perfectly built-in excuse, "I hit that ball exactly where I wanted to. I completely forgot there was a bunker there."

## *"These fairways are too narrow."*

One great thing about golf is that no two courses are the same, and there are literally thousands to choose from. Thus, if you take advantage of the selection by trying something new, there's a chance that you might accidentally choose to play on a demanding course (or, perhaps worse, some-one selects an arduous course for you). If you are known for spraying your tee shots, before your next round starts, make sure to let your group know that you like to really go for it off the tee. It's go big or go home. However, due to your macho playing style at times you will find the rough off of the tee. Then, when the expected occurs and you miss the fairway, just hit them with, "Due to my big game, I need a wide-open course. These fairways are just too narrow for my manly game."

### "That putt would have gone in if it didn't hit a pebble."

Okay, so you're not a great putter. You three- or four-putt on a regular basis, and you've never seen a three-footer that you couldn't blow. If this sounds like you, don't worry, there's hope. Make sure to complain early and often about the poor condition of the course—especially the greens. You're clearly an excellent golfer and can only play well under pristine conditions. Then, when you botch an easy putt just say, "Did you see that? My putt was right on line until it hit a pebble. The grounds crew really ought to be fired."

## *"This is my first round of the season."*

True . . . you love golf and will play at any opportunity you can. You play every weekend you can, and you've even been known to wake up early before work to get a few holes in (but don't worry, that will be our secret). Nevertheless, if it's also true that despite playing constantly, taking lessons, going to the range, reading about the sport, and watching the golf channel, you're still a terrible golfer, rest assured that you're not alone. But this embarrassing fact doesn't have to make you look like the unathletic fool that you are. Before your round, let everyone know that you've been so busy with work, your family, blah, blah, blah that you haven't been able to make it out for a round this year. Then, if you play well, great. You can chalk it up to your superior natural ability. But in the likely event that you score in the triple digits, the excuse is right there for the taking: "I know I didn't play well, but what can you expect? This was, after all, my first round of the season."

## *"I hit a branch during my backswing."*

One of the many things I like about the great game of golf is the ability to get creative. Sure, it's easier to hit from the middle of the fairway. But what happens when you're in a bit

of trouble and have to get out of Dodge to save your par? If you've been known to have to scramble from time to time, notify your group that this is a strong point of your game. You really thrive on the ingenuity of the difficult situation. Then, if you find yourself in the woods and have to pull a Houdini act to save par, you'll have a built-in excuse if things don't go as planned. If you blunder your shot try saying, "I would have definitely ended up on the green if I didn't hit a branch during my backswing. . . what bad luck."

> ### Did You Know?
> *Eighty percent of all golfers will never achieve a handicap of lower than 18.*

### "The pin placements were unusually hard."

As I've mentioned previously, one of the great things about golf is that no two courses are identical. There are so many great courses to choose from, and each one is like a new adventure. But even if you play your home course over and over again, the tee box can change, the rough may get a little longer at times, and of course the pin placements can change. If you're a poor putter, make sure to set up your round by telling your comrades that you've heard that the pin placements today are like the US Open on Sundays. Then, when you miss putt after putt, you can let your friends know, "I would have scored much better if it weren't for those unusually difficult pin placements."

## *"I need to focus more on my short game."*

We've all heard it: "Drive for show, putt for dough." But regardless, many of us seem to go to the range and bomb drives and long irons for hours, only to neglect our short games. Make sure to let your fellow golfers know that you simply haven't had the time to work on your short game lately. Then, when you chip it off the green, or miss a short putt, simply come back with, "I just need to focus a bit more on my short game. Then I'll surely be shooting in the 70s again."

## *"I don't like playing this early/late."*

Are you an early riser? A night owl? Or do you hit your stride

during midday? Because we all have our own preferences, you can use this to your advantage. Even if you're playing at your ideal time, there's no harm in keeping that information to yourself. If you have an early or late tee time, come in yawning and pretend to rub the sleep out of your eyes. Before the round, make sure to tell anyone who will listen that your tee time conflicts with your circadian rhythms. Then, if you play well, no harm done. But in the likely event that your form holds true, and you butcher the course like a piece of meat, the reliable excuse is there, "Thanks for the round, but I'm really just not a morning/night person."

## *"My dog chewed a hole in my favorite golf shoes."*

Finding the right equipment can be essential to a good golf game. We've all seen the player who has used the same putter for about 50 years and won't give it up. And this holds true not only for your clubs but for your clothing as well. Consequently, if you notice around hole five or six that you're likely to end up on the losing end of the round, I would suggest you start to walk gingerly. Bend down and take your shoes on and off several times. Then, re-tie your shoelaces. Then, when there is nothing left for you to do but buy the drinks, you might want to say something like, "Nice round.

It's too bad that my dog chewed a hole in my favorite golf shoes. This new pair was killing my feet."

## *"My ball was sitting halfway on the fairway and halfway on the rough."*

As previously mentioned, golf is a game that takes immense skill. But of course, as every golfer is well too aware, a bit of luck comes into the contest as well. If you're noticing that your iron game is going down the tubes, don't despair. The next time your ball lands anywhere near the rough, block your partner's view with your body. Then sigh heavily and complain about your lack of good fortune. But make sure to walk up to the ball and hit it quickly before your friends can get a better look. And if your form holds true, and you hit another duck of a shot, just say, "I can't believe my bad luck. The ball was sitting on the lip of the fairway and the rough. I just can't catch a break!"

## *"This area shouldn't be considered out of bounds."*

Of course, you love the great game of golf. You think about it, dream about it, and relish the chance to play. But that doesn't mean you're any good at it. Putting is difficult, your short game is horrendous, and most of all you spray your drives and long irons like a sprinkler system on a windy day. So at the beginning of the round, make sure to complain about the narrow course. You've always been a fan of the courses in Ireland and Britain where it's wide open. Then, when sure enough you hit one astray, just say, "I really don't think that this area should be out of bounds. I have a clear shot to the pin from here."

### *"I left my pitching wedge somewhere on the front nine."*

If you're in match play, and you're getting your "you know what" handed to you, well . . . desperate times, desperate measures. When you find yourself down four holes at the turn, discretely leave your pitching wedge near the green at the turn. Don't worry, surely someone will pick it up and turn it in to the pro shop. Then, when the carnage is over, shake hands with your opponent and tell them, "Good match. I just wish I didn't lose my pitching wedge. I really can't play without it."

### *"One of my shoelaces broke, and now my shoe is too loose."*

Your game is a mess, and there is no salvaging your round. You're facing triple digits, and the embarrassment meter is through the roof. When no one is looking, take something sharp out of your bag and cut one of your shoelaces. If you don't have anything sharp, take off your shoe and use your teeth . . . sometimes you gotta do what you gotta do. Then, after the round, show your shoe to your opponent and say, "I just couldn't play well with this broken shoelace. My foot felt like it was going to come right out of my shoe on every shot." If it can work for Tonya Harding in the Olympics, it can surely work for you.

### *"My knees were bent too much, and I got under the ball."*

Okay, so you've been known to take divots that can rival NY City potholes. Before you start to chew up the turf, let your fellow golfers know that the club pro has advised you to bend your knees more. The pro is sure that this will improve your game, and who are you to question a qualified professional? But then, when your divot goes further than the ball, you have a built-in excuse. "I was trying to heed the advice of my

club pro. But clearly I'm too good of a student. I'm obviously bending my knees too much and getting under the ball."

### Did You Know?

*Many US presidents have been avid golfers. But I submit that President Woodrow Wilson leads the list. President Wilson was so devoted to the sport that he used to play in the snow using black golf balls.*

### *"If it weren't for bad luck I'd have no luck at all."*

Sure, golf is a game that requires immense skill and talent. But sometimes, it takes a little bit of luck as well. If your game is in the toilet, you can use this acumen to your advantage. So you've had three double bogeys on the back nine and you're about to tear up your golf card and throw your clubs in the lake. But just wait a minute, your terrible round can't be all your fault. Let's remember that you're an exceptional athlete, a great golfer, and quite good-looking as well. Before the round finishes, make sure to comment on some of the bad bounces you've received. Then you might want to throw in that the wind changed directions at the last minute and a bird chirped right in your backswing. And when the round is mercifully over, sum it up with, "If it weren't for bad luck, I'd have no luck at all."

### *"I normally play with a mulligan per hole."*

There are lots of ways to lose at golf, and just as many excuses as to why you did. This one is admittedly pathetic, but what the heck. Nobody ever accused you (or me) of sucking up a loss without whining. So as they say, "Whatever works." You're in a handicap tournament, licking your chops because you have prepared by stealthily chunking chips and blowing easy putts for several rounds in order to raise your personal handicap by six strokes. But unfortunately for you, your opponents are even more devious than you are, so it turns out that you're in an uphill struggle against tricksters who have been around the block a lot more times than you have.

At the beginning of the round, bring up the possibility of mulligans. Surely, your opponent will tell you that this is not allowed during tournament play. And if the inevitable occurs, and you go down in defeat, it will be doubly hard to take, because not only did you get outplayed, you were also outhustled. But by no means do you walk away without having the last word to the guy who won. "I'm not accusing you of anything, but that 22 handicap of yours just doesn't compute with your score of 79. Plus, my usual playing partners are a lot nicer than you. They normally give me a mulligan per hole."

### *"The ball was above my feet, but it didn't hook."*

One thing that makes golf so difficult is that no two shots are exactly alike. And if you find yourself in a precarious position on the course, things can be doubly difficult. As any astute golfer knows, if the ball ends up above your feet, it should hook. If you find yourself in just such a position, before you hit, you need to let everyone watching know of the situation at hand. Then, if your shot doesn't end up snuggling up to the hole, it surely wouldn't be your fault. Just explain it with, "I don't know what happened. You all saw it. The ball was above my feet. I have no idea why it didn't hook and end up right on the green."

## *"I was distracted by the ugly outfit my partner was wearing."*

One of the many enjoyable things about golf are the outrageous outfits that many players wear. Unlike tennis, where lily whites are at times required, plaid and bright colors rule the day on the course. But if you're playing poorly, you can use this to your advantage as well. Make sure to comment on the atrocious shirt/pants/hat, etc. that your fellow golfer is wearing. You might even want to lay it on thick and say that their look is hurting your eyes. Then, if you end up on the losing side of the scorecard, explain it with, "I was so distracted by my partner's outfit that I simply couldn't focus on my game."

## *"I've never played on a course with the rough so thick."*

As previously mentioned, one great thing about golf is that no two courses are identical. And there are so many fantastic courses out there. But if you're playing a course for the first time (or even if it's your hundredth time . . . I won't tell) and things are going well, start to complain loudly about the course conditions. You might want to mention that they're nothing like those of your home course. Then, after your

lousy round, you can blame it on the following. "I've never played on a course with a rough so thick. This is preposterous. What is this . . . the US Open?!"

### "I still don't have a feel for these new clubs."

Everyone knows that change is hard. It even takes the professionals time to get used to their new equipment. And you can use this information to your advantage. The next time your game starts to go off the rails, make sure to show off your new clubs. Tell them you just purchased this new set. You're sure it will improve your game in the long run, but it's going to take a while to get used to them. Then, after a miserable round, just say, "The next time we play, I'll surely be much better. But for now, I still don't have a feel for my new clubs."

### "I always play poorly when we play together."

Let's say you're out playing with your regular partner who, on a regular basis, seems to beat you like you stole their paycheck. You're sick of losing all the time, but what can you do? Well, I say, dear friend . . . read on. Make sure to drop a hint or two that you don't know why, but somehow you always seem to lose concentration when you play together. Perhaps it's due to his or her devilish good looks or winning personality, but you just can't seem to play up to your normal, exceptional ability when you play with him or her. Then, when the inevitable happens, and you lose yet again, just say, "It's the strangest thing, I just always play so poorly when we play together."

### *"My golf bag is too heavy . . . I'm exhausted."*

To be honest, usually when I play golf I take a cart. But from time to time I get inspired to get a little exercise, and I'll take that beautiful, long walk in nature for 18 holes. Sure it can be tiring, but it can be exhilarating as well. Plus, you can use it to your advantage. If your game starts to fall apart, begin to huff and puff as you walk. Then, when the bloodbath is over, just look your fellow golfers straight in the eye and say, "This golf bad feels like it weighs a ton. I could barely make it through the round. I'm exhausted."

## "I keep dropping my left shoulder and hooking the ball."

Nothing makes you happier than your weekend golf game, but recently you've been off form. For some reason, you've been hooking the ball like a bowler trying to pick up a 7-10 split and can't seem to straighten things out. Clearly, this can't be your fault and must be due to some hiccup in the universe. So when you're out for a round with your buddies, and you've hit three drives into the woods, start to massage your upper arm. Then, when you have everyone's attention, begin to stretch out your shoulder. And finally, after your utter collapse, just say, "This old football injury is acting up again. I just can't seem to stop dropping my left shoulder and hooking the ball."

## "I would have shot my age if I was forty years older."

There are several major accomplishments in this great sport that every golfer aspires to. Breaking 80 and a hole in one come to mind. And then, of course, there is shooting your age. To implement this excuse properly, the first thing you'll want to do is to find some older playing partners. Let them know that although you may be younger than them, you've got an old soul. And if you're not playing well, make sure to mention that you've only been playing for a short amount of time. Throw out the fact that once you're their age, you'll surely be a better golfer. Then, when you score in the 90s, hit 'em with, "If I were a couple of decades older I would have shot my age."

## Did You Know?

In the early days of golf, some of the first golf balls were made exclusively from hardwood such as box trees and beech. These wooden balls would typically only last for a few rounds. And for the golfer who didn't fancy the wood version, an alternative and more expensive option was a "feathery," which was a ball filled with chicken or goose feathers and enclosed in a leathery pouch.

## "I had a bad lie."

We've all heard it: "Better to be lucky than good." At one point or another, it applies to all of us, so why not use it to your advantage? If you're not playing well, start to complain about how unlucky you've been all around. Your putts have been lipping out all day, and at one point a gopher actually ran away with your ball. So the next time you shank a shot like there's no tomorrow, just chalk it up to, "Wow, my bad luck today is uncanny. I just had the worst lie."

### *"I was set up too close/far away from the ball."*

We've all been there. You're standing over the ball and you just don't feel comfortable. If your game is starting to fall apart, you might want to begin by mentioning that your vertigo has been acting up. You've been feeling dizzy all day and are having trouble with your balance. Then, when you shank a shot, just mention "It's so hard to set up properly when I feel so dizzy. Once again I was too close/far from the ball."

### *"I thought that par 4 was a par 5 and I was laying up."*

Okay, so you're not the biggest hitter, but you can always rely on your fantastic short game to get you through the round. Yet your macho playing partners are always bragging about how far they can blast it, and you feel left out. So of course, in order to keep up with the Joneses, you tell your friends that you regularly go 275 off the tee and can hit your nine-iron about 160. Then, when the rubber hits the road, and you're 50 yards short of the green, you'll be in a perfect situation to say, "I thought that hole was a par 5 and I was laying up."

### *"I've been playing so well recently that I was overconfident."*

I love this excuse. Of course you've been scoring in the 70s recently, and you'll tell everyone who will listen that your handicap is in the single digits. But when you get out onto the course, it's difficult to hide how poorly you're playing. At this point make sure to tell your foursome that it's just so hard to understand how you're 15 over par at the turn because you've been playing so well. Then, as the horror continues, make sure to repeatedly shake your head in utter disbelief. And when the round mercifully ends, you can say, "Wow, golf really is a cruel sport. I guess after my last couple of stellar rounds, I was just overconfident."

### "I have terrific form. I just don't score well."

Sure, you're a natural athlete. Sports have just always come easily to you. So why is golf so gosh darn hard?! The next time you're out "enjoying" a round with your friends, make sure to tell them about your recent lesson. Let them know that the pro couldn't stop commenting on your beautiful swing. Although you're not positive, you vaguely remember the club professional mentioning something about a Greek god. Then, when the misery has ended, you can justify your ballooning scorecard with, "I may not have scored as well as the others, but I'm sure you would kill to have my form."

### "I just picked up this sport."

As we all know, golf is, to say the least, a difficult game to master. Most of us play the sport for years and don't ever get close to shooting par. Even if you've been playing for a while, make sure to tell your foursome that you're new to the sport. You may even want to mention that this is one of the first rounds you've ever played. And if you want to really be devious, you can ask if anyone wants to put a little wager on the round . . . you've heard that it is fun to bet a few dollars. Then, when you shoot in the 90s, you can collect a few bucks and have a built-in excuse as well. "I just picked up golf. I'm sure I'll be better the next time."

## "All this sun has dried out the greens. The ball is rolling way faster than normal."

One of the things I like most about this great sport is playing on a beautiful summer day. With the birds chirping and the sun shining, it is a great way to feel at one with nature. But of course that picturesque day can turn into a bit of a nightmare if your game goes off the rails—especially if you lose your touch on the greens. So the next time you're putting like you've lost all feeling in your hands, start to complain about how hot it is. Then mention how dry the course seems to be. You might even want to mention that it appears as if the course hasn't been watered in days. And finally, when you've four-putted yet again, you can explain it with, "These greens are completely dried out. Where are we, at the US Open?!"

## *"I've never played this course before."*

Sure, you regularly score in the triple digits. You couldn't get out of a sand trap if your life depended on it, and you have about as much natural talent as a gnat. But if you're playing a course for the first time, or if you're playing with a new foursome and you've actually played the course several times before (don't worry, I won't tell), try the following. Throughout the round, ask about the course layout. For example, "Is there a bunker up ahead?", "Where is the pin placement on the next hole?", etc. Then, when the round is over, try this on for size, "This is the first time I've ever played this course. When I play it again, I'll surely score better."

## *"I'm in between clubs."*

If I'm being honest (which is a rarity in this book), half the time I have no idea how far my shots are going to go. I'm just as likely to chunk a fairway iron as I am to riffle it over the green. But once again, that will be our secret. If you find yourself in the ever too common position of complete befuddlement on the course, start to stand over your shots, shake your head back and forth, look pensive, and then return to your bag. Grab a different club and start the ritual all over again. Then, at the end of the round, when your scorecard reads scarier than a Stephen King novel, you can say, "It was just the strangest thing. I was in between clubs all day. What bad luck."

### *"My club face was open/closed."*

In my humble opinion, one of the reasons why golf is such a difficult sport is that so many things can go wrong. There are just so many moving parts. So if you've been known to hook your shots like Peter Pan's nemesis, or slice like your neighborhood butcher, make sure to tell your friends that you've been working with your club professional. Mention that the pro has changed your grip and you're having difficulty getting used to your new swing. Then, when the inevitable happens, and you hit another errant shot, follow it up with, "I just can't get used to the new grip. My club face was too open/closed again."

## Did You Know?

Like to play a quick 18 holes? Well, Alice Miller holds the current LPGA Tour record for the fastest round. Miller polished off her 18-hole final round of the 1997 Welch's/Circle K Championship in a lightning-fast one hour, 26 minutes, and 44 seconds.

### *"I can't seem to get comfortable over the ball."*

It's been said that golf is primarily a mental sport. You need to have supreme confidence in order to play at a top level. If you believe it, you can achieve it. But there are those times when no matter how hard you are trying to concentrate, your game just won't cooperate. For these times, make sure to mention what a bad night sleep you've had. Or perhaps you can throw in that you've recently had a lot of pressure at work. Then, stand over your ball, sigh heavily, and take a step back. Repeat this routine several times per hole if need be. Then, after another blowup hole, just state, "I don't know what's going on. I just can't seem to get comfortable over the ball."

## *"I was hitting 'em great on the range."*

It's been said that pressure kills. And this statement has never been truer than on the golf course. So make sure you get to the course well before your tee-time. Make sure everyone knows that you've been honing your skills on the range. Then, if your game melts down like Chernobyl, put a look of utter disbelief on your face. And when the painstaking round comes to an end, just tell 'em. "I have no idea what just happened out there. I mean, I was hitting them great on the range."

## *"I tried to put backspin on it."*

There are literally thousands of golfers in the world, but only a handful can truly master the game. When to hit a draw or a fade, consistently getting out of a trap easily, rarely three-putting. These are just a few of the many examples of what separates the average golfer from the exceptional. And of course there is the skill of putting backspin on the ball. In my humble opinion, this is another distinction between good and great. But if you're merely an average golfer, you can use the concept of backspin to your advantage. Tell all of your fellow golfers that you've been working with your club pro on bringing your already terrific game to the next level. Then, when you fail to get on green after green in regulation, you'll have a perfect excuse set up. Just tell your buddies, "I was trying to put backspin on my approaches all day. Once I get the hang of it, I'll be unstoppable."

### *"A fly landed on my ball during my downswing."*

It goes without saying that golf is a very difficult sport. Perhaps that's why it brings such satisfaction when you're playing well. But of course, it can also lead to immense frustration when that little white dimpled ball isn't acting according to plan. So in an effort to have more good days than bad, you need truly to focus on the task at hand. Any little loss of attention can lead to a monumental breakdown. If you find that you're having an off day, well surely you don't want to admit that it's your fault (why else would you be reading this book?)! First, when you have everyone's attention, complain about all of the little gnats on the course. Then, wave your hand in front of your face like you're trying to shoo away those pesky insects. And finally, when you really hit a whopper of a bad shot, follow it up with, "A darn fly landed on my ball right during my downswing. It completely ruined my concentration."

### *"These greens are harder/softer than I thought."*

I've said it before, and I'll say it again: Drive for show, Putt for dough. It's all well and good if you can hit a 300-yard drive, but if you follow it up with a couple of three putts, you're still not going to score very well. If you're having one of those days where you've completely lost your touch on the greens, start by complaining about the weather conditions. Too hot, too cold, too humid, too windy . . . feel free to come up with any of your own as well. Then, when your putt doesn't come anywhere near the hole, just tell your playing partner, "These greens are way harder/softer than I thought. How am I supposed to putt under these conditions?!"

### "I thought the pin was in the front/back of the green."

If you're like most of the golfers I know, you're just happy if your ball lands in the general vicinity of your target. But once again, that can be our secret. As far as you let your friends know, you are an excellent golfer, a true patriot, and an extremely generous tipper to boot. So the next time you're losing your friendly golf wager, begin by rubbing your eyes. If you wear glasses, take them off and examine them closely. If you don't, you may want to feign losing one of your contacts. Then, when you're lucky enough to land your ball on the green, don't look too happy. Put a disgusted look on your face and say, "My eyes have been bothering me all day today. I thought that pin was in the front/back of the green."

### "That shot would have been perfect if I had used one club more/less."

I've been playing golf for years, and to be perfectly honest half of the time I feel like I have absolutely no idea what I'm doing. And that goes for the length of my shots as well. But alas, at least I've come up with a good excuse to cover myself, which I'm happy to share. First, make sure to mention that you don't know the course you are playing on very well. Then, you might want to bring up the fact that you usually play with a caddy—besides being a great golfer, you're extremely rich as well. Lastly, when you miss the green by a country mile just follow it up with, "That shot would have been pin-high if I had just used one more/less club."

## *"Golf is just an unfair sport."*

As we all are well too aware, golf is hard enough on a normal day. But when the golf gods are against you, it can lead to a miserable round. For example, on some days, it just seems like everything is going wrong. Your ball kicks off a tree and goes out of bounds. Or your perfect drive down the middle of the fairway lands right in a divot. But whether your game is suffering due to bad luck, or your own ineptitude, make sure to use this tried and true excuse. First, mumble to yourself loudly that nothing seems to be going right. If you're really bold, you might even want to look up to the heavens and cry out, "Why God, why?!" Then, when your round is over, just look your friends square in the eye and say, "I really didn't play that poorly today. Golf can just truly just be an unfair sport."

## *"My golf shoes are hurting my feet."*

In the early 1990s, Spike Lee and Michael Jordan teamed together in a successful ad campaign for Nike where Lee's character was famous for saying, "It's gotta be the shoes." In my opinion, this motto also pertains to the great game of golf. Sometimes, a good pair of shoes with just the right spikes can truly be helpful. But what happens when your shoes are anything but advantageous? Well, fear not because I have just the excuse for you. If you're not playing up to par (pun intended), take off your shoes and rub your feet. Then, make sure to walk gingerly around the course whenever you're in eyeshot of your playing partners. And when the round ends and you're left holding the bag, just say, "How can I expect to play well when my golf shoes have been killing my feet all day?"

## *"I should have gone with my first instinct."*

Should I go with a five iron or six? To lay up or go for the green? Does that putt break to the left or right? Golf, like life, is full of decisions. But why does it always seem like

I'm making the wrong choices on the course? Well, at least now you can use this to your advantage. After each poor shot, make sure to sigh loudly and yell out, "I knew it!" You may even want to make several trips to your bag before each important shot. Then, if your round ends predictably poorly, just say, "Why am I always second-guessing myself? I really need to go with my first instincts."

### Did You Know?

The legend Sam Snead is the only male golfer to chalk up a victory on the LPGA Tour. Snead pulled off the feat when he took home the trophy at the 1962 Royal Poinciana Plaza Invitational with a five-shot margin of victory.

### "My feet weren't parallel to the hole."

In my opinion, one of the many reasons that golf is so difficult is that there is just so much to remember. *Keep your head still. Hit down on the ball. Make a good turn.* And that's just the tip of the iceberg. So the next time your game is falling apart, make sure to hit the front of your head with the palm of your hand. Then yell out, "concentrate, you fool!" And finally, when you find your shots going wayward, just tell your group, "Why is it that I just can't seem to keep my feet parallel to the hole?"

## *"I just couldn't recover after going six over on the first three holes."*

Golf is a funny game. You can have the worst round, but that one good shot will keep you coming back and craving more. And as I've often heard, "A bad day of golf is surely better than a good day at work." So if you're having one of those days, and nothing seems to be going right, wait until you hit that one decent shot. Then tell your comrades that you've finally got it all figured out. And when you're tailing up your pathetic score, just say, "I got it all working at the end. I'll score much better next time. Too bad I just couldn't recover from my horrendous start."

## *"I can't putt well with my new putter."*

As I've mentioned several times in this book, it doesn't matter how well your long game is if you can't putt. As it has often been said, a missed three-foot putt counts the same as your huge drive. So, what's the remedy? Many golfers will practice until the cows come home. But if you're anything like me, you may be inclined to try and buy yourself a better game. In that case, what happens when you spend your hard-earned cash on a new putter only to have the same dismal results? Well, not to worry. First, after a poor putt, examine your club. Let your fellow golfers know that this is a brand-new club, and this is the first time you've played with it (What . . . it's your 20th time? That will be our secret.) Then, after you've consistently three- and even four-putted your way through the round, hold your head up high and say, "I just can't play well with this new putter. I'm sure I'll be back to one- and two-putting once I get used to it."

## *"A bunch of hackers ahead of us ruined the greens."*

Because you are clearly a phenomenal golfer, you need and expect the best in terms of equipment, circumstances, and of course golf etiquette. I mean, how can you play up to your exquisite standards without the proper conditions? So the next time your putter fails you, get down on your hands and knees as if you're carefully examining the greens. Then, stare at the group ahead of you and start to mutter under your breath about those "SOBs." And finally, when your round is over and you're looking for a way to clarify the damage, try explaining it with, "Those damn hackers ahead of us have completely ruined the greens."

## "I can't gauge my distance if I don't know the altitude."

For many of us, we just grip it and rip it and try to enjoy the moment. But for others, they examine every intricacy of the game. And clearly, because you are a master golfer, the latter applies to you. So the next time your ball isn't landing anywhere near the green, ask your comrades if anyone knows exactly how many feet above sea level the course is. When you receive the expected, "I have no idea, dude" response, just shake your head in disbelief. Then, at the end of the day when you end up holding the short end of the stick, just shoot back with, "I just don't understand how I'm expected to gauge the distance when I don't know the exact altitude."

## *"I played that shot too far back/forward in my stance."*

So you've been playing for years and still generally have no idea what the hell you're doing on a golf course. Well, I say, join the club! But alas, that's yet another reason why you desperately need this book. If you're one of the many golfers that just addresses the ball and prays, try this on for size. First, when you stand over your shot, shuffle your feet forward and backward several times. Step away from the ball, come back, and then repeat. After yet another shot goes wayward, just explain it with, "I definitely played that shot too far back/forward in my stance . . . what was I thinking?!"

## *"Now that I'm older, I've developed a case of the yips."*

As I've often heard, "Father Time is undefeated." However, getting older can come with some advantages as well, and I'm not just talking about the senior citizen discounts. As some of the more mature golfers will attest, from time to time they may encounter a case of the yips on the greens. But I say, why not use this to your advantage? First, make sure to let everyone know how difficult it is to play at your advanced age. If you increase the number a few years don't worry— I won't tell. Then, after you miss several putts inside of three feet, look at your fellow golfers with pride and say, "I may be wiser now that I'm older, but it's hard to score well with this case of the yips."

## *"Your ball marker distracted me."*

I believe I've made it abundantly clear that golf is a very difficult game. Clearly, the only way to play well is to devote all of your concentration into each and every shot. Even the professionals will complain when their concentration is interrupted, so why can't you? If you're on the green and staring down a difficult shot, make sure to ask your fellow golfer to mark their ball. But after they do so, sigh heavily and shake your head. Then, if the inevitable occurs, and your putt doesn't end up anywhere near the hole, look your playing partner straight in the eye and say, "I always make a putt of this distance, but I was distracted by your pretentious ball marker."

## "The range ran out of balls and I couldn't warm-up properly."

As any good boy scout will attest, you need to be prepared. And the best way to get ready to play a solid round of golf, in my opinion, is to have a nice long warm-up on the range. But if your game has gone to hell, make sure to mutter under your breath about how unreliable the course is. Then, when the round is over and you find yourself buying the drinks, just say, "I don't know how I was supposed to play well today. The range ran out of balls in the middle of my warm-up, and I was completed unprepared to play up to my usual exceptional standards."

## "I keep taking the club back too quickly."

As many golf professionals have told me, a nice smooth club takeback is the key to setting up a well-struck ball. So why in the world is that so hard to remember? But once again, I say, 'Why not use this to your advantage?' If you're struggling with your woods and/or irons, make sure to tell your group that you've got a lot on your mind. You may also want to add that your club professional gave you some really good tips, but your brain is so full that you can't seem to remember a thing that they told you. Then, after your round mercifully comes to an end, just say, "Ah . . . now I remember, I was taking the club back too quickly."

## Did You Know?

*The longest putt ever made in tournament golf was recorded at the 1976 International Four-Ball Pro Am when Bob Cook sunk a 140-foot, 2¾-inch putt on the 18th hole at St. Andrews.*

## "I really need a drink and haven't seen the beer cart all day."

Okay, I admit it! One of my favorite parts of the round is taking a long swig of a cold one. But if you happen to have the misfortune of missing the beer cart, start to clear your throat repeatedly. Tell your friends how dry your mouth is. You might even mention that you may pass out from dehydration. Then, if your round doesn't finish as well as you had hoped, just say, "I really needed a beer. How in the world am I supposed to play well when I've been parched all round?!"

## *"My lesson was rained out this week."*

We've all heard that practice makes perfect. But what happens on those days when you're not even close to perfect? The first thing you need to do is to look up to the heavens and complain about the terrible weather you've been having. Then mention that it's been a really long time since you've had a chance to meet with your club professional. And finally, when your miserable round has humanely come to an end, just tell your fellow golfers that, "This weather has been god-awful and my lesson was rained out again. How can I be expected to keep up with my normally superb play without the proper instruction?"

## *"I meant to lag that putt."*

As I've mentioned throughout this book, putting well is essential to a quality round. But what happens if your sweet putting stroke has eluded you? First, tell your friends that you've been feeling some tingling in your extremities. While you can't be positive, it's possible that you're losing the feeling in your hands. Then, the next time you hit your putt well past the hole, put a bewildered look on your face and say, "I just don't know what's happening. I meant to lag that putt. Perhaps I should drive myself to the hospital . . . but after the round of course."

## *"I can't make a full enough turn now that I'm over 50."*

As my father used to tell me when I was a child, and I've learned all too well now that I'm an adult, it's tough getting old. But there is good news. Golf is a lifetime sport, and many play well into their nineties. But of course, scoring well into your old age is another challenge altogether. If you're getting up there in age, start by complaining about how sore your muscles are. Then, make sure to bend down very slowly when picking up your tee after your drive. And finally, if you're playing with younger golfers look those young pups straight in the eye and say, "When I was your age I would have whipped you into tomorrow. But now that I'm older I just can't make a full enough turn to score like I used to."

### *"I thought that tree was smaller than it actually is."*

In the golfing world, it's been well stated that trees are 90 percent air. Yet despite that fact, any golfer worth their salt will try to avoid these natural obstacles whenever possible. However, try as we may, there are going to be times where we find ourselves in the precarious position of having to hit around, or even through, a tree. If you find yourself in just such a situation, make sure to rub your eyes. If you're wearing glasses, take them off and examine them for a bit. Then, if your shot ends up finding one of nature's beasts, you can easily state, "That tree looked much smaller than it actually is."

### *"Your shadow distracted me."*

I've said it before, and I'll say it again: golf takes extreme concentration to play at the highest level. Any minor distraction can lead to disaster on the course. So if the sun is out and you're standing over a difficult shot, look around and sigh heavily. Step away from the ball and mutter to yourself about how some people are just so inconsiderate. Then, if you blunder your stroke, look the closest golfer to you straight in the eye and say, "Your shadow distracted me. Would it be asking too much for a little golf etiquette?"

## *"Someone walked on my through line."*

Obviously (*ahem*), you're an exceptional golfer. And because you're the best, you expect nothing but the best. From the most exquisite courses to the most pristine equipment, nothing is too good for you. And of course, this holds true for the rules of etiquette as well. Most golfers know not to walk between a golfer's ball on the green and the hole. But not all golfers understand not to walk past the hole as well. If this dastardly occurrence takes place, give the culprit your best "dagger eyes." Then, if your putt goes past the hole, start to mutter under your breath about how some people are just so gosh darn inconsiderate. And finally, if you miss the comebacker, in your most indignant voice say, "Unreal, I can't believe you actually walked in my through line."

## *"I don't play well with this brand of golf ball."*

While most of your average golfers don't know the difference between golf balls, you of course take the decision of what brand to use very seriously. For you are a superior athlete, and the type of ball can make all of the difference for your finely tuned game. But what happens when your game deserts you? First, ask one of your playing partners for a ball and thank them graciously. But then, if your round doesn't improve, after you've finished up on the 18th hole, take a close look at the ball and say, "Of course . . . now it makes sense why I played so poorly. I never play well with this brand of ball."

### *"You weren't paying attention to all of my good shots."*

So your round isn't going according to plan. Your game is blowing up right in front of you, and to make matters worse, your buddies are riding you like a horse at the Kentucky Derby. But alas, not to worry. First, tell them that you're actually scoring decently well. I won't tell if you turn that "8" into a "4" on your scorecard. Then, when the round is over, and your friends insist that, as the loser, you buy the drinks, you can say, "Not so fast. I actually came in first. You all simply weren't paying attention to all of my many good shots."

## "My grips are too slick from sweating."

If you ask me, the best seasons to play golf are in the spring and fall. Too many humid days during the dog days of summer, and before you know it, good luck on holding on to the club because the grips are soaked from your sweaty hands. So unless you have a waterproof glove, and a couple pairs of replacements as well, you might as well be holding onto a slippery eel when you're trying to make a decent swing. Needless to say, this is a built-in excuse for playing badly. And even if your clubs aren't really full of sweat, don't worry . . . I won't tell. Just pour some water on your grips and make sure everyone can see how soaked they are. And if it really is hot, your playing partners will be challenged under these circumstances as well. But if they somehow manage to shoot a decent score, all you have to say is, "You guys must have better gloves than I do. My grips felt like they fell in a bathtub."

### Did You Know?

In 2010, fervent golfer Richard Lewis played an eye-popping 11,000 holes to set the one-year record. And incredibly, Lewis played each and every hole at the Four Seasons Resort and Club in Irving, Texas.

## *"I keep forgetting to hit down on the ball."*

As much as I try, I just can't figure out why I love golf so much. It can be so immensely frustrating, and yet I can't get it out of my mind. The more I play, the more I realize how much more there is that can go wrong. It's just so hard to keep everything straight in my noggin. So I suggest just to fess up. Start up a conversation about the perils of golf and how hard it is to play this seemingly easy game. Surely your buddies will nod their heads knowingly. Then, when you botch another iron shot, just admit, "Once again I forgot to hit down on the ball. I'm sure you can certainly understand."

## *"The trap wasn't raked properly."*

You may have heard the joke about the guy who said he couldn't get out of traps, but the first time he hit a sand shot it landed inches from the hole. His opponent was astounded and said, "I thought you said you couldn't get out of traps!" To which the guy responded by reaching out his arm for assistance and pleading, "I can't. Please pull me out of here!"

Most of us can manage physically to walk out of a sand trap, but while doing so we're muttering some excuse as to why we just flubbed the shot. To set this up, make sure you let your playing partners know that you require a meticulous course. Your game is clearly so well-tuned that one out of place blade of grass can make a difference. Then, when you start swatting in the trap like you're digging for water in the desert, that's the time to rely on the age-old excuse: "Damn! Someone before us didn't rake this trap. Otherwise, I would have been right on that pin!"

### "All of my recent weightlifting has thrown off my golf swing."

Clearly you hit the gym often. Sure, you might not have the kind of showy muscles of a professional athlete, but hell yeah . . . you're as strong as an ox. If your game is going straight downhill, make sure to tell your compatriots that you came to the course straight from the gym. You're actually a little disappointed because you only benched 350 pounds today (You usually put up at least 400). But then, after you finish a miserable round, just tell your foursome, "It's really hard to play well when I've been pumping so much iron."

## *"My swing speed is off."*

If you're playing with some serious golfers and need an intricate excuse, try this one on for size. First, let your group know that you've been working to take your game to the next level. The club pro says you have enormous potential, but that you might have to take a step backward before you make that major leap forward. And finally, after your next epic failure of a round, just say, "My swing speed was really off today. Once I find the right timing I'll be unstoppable."

## *"It's too cold/hot."*

There are few things more enjoyable than playing golf on a pristine day. But what about those days when the weather gods just aren't cooperating? Well, I guess you could just stay home . . . not! But you can use the unseemly conditions to your favor. First, make sure to do a lot of complaining—"It's freezing out here!" or "I'm melting it's so hot!" And then, after braving the elements, as you're enjoying a beverage at the 19th hole, tell your friends, "How could I expect to play well today? It was just way too cold/hot!"

## *"I was standing too close/far from the ball."*

It's one of those days. You can't get comfortable while stand-ing over the ball, even though your stance is exactly the same as it has been for a hundred previous rounds. So, it's not your positioning. Something has gone off with your swing, you're spraying shots all over the golf course, and it's getting to be embarrassing. You can forget about trying to fix the problem while you're playing. You'll need to spend some time with a pro to figure it out, but in the meantime, you've got to come up with some way to save face. Here's your solution: While addressing the ball, back away a few inches and take an exaggerated reach with your club. You'll surely screw up the shot, but your partners will at least notice that you're trying to modify your stance. Then, the next time, move for-ward so that you're too close to the ball. Repeat this process a few times, and it will also help to tap the side of your head as though you're trying to clear some water from your ear. This will set you up with an excuse for playing like a beginner. "I just couldn't find the right distance with my stance today. Must have a virus in my middle ear or something. Every time I approached the ball I was standing either too close or too far away."

## *"It's way too humid to play well."*

Give me the springtime or fall for the ideal round of golf. Nothing like a cool, crisp day to concentrate on the game and direct that little white ball to exactly where you want it to go. The problem is that summer is the height of the golf season, and even if you don't live in the tropics, there are those hot days that can make you feel like you're in a sauna. But maybe there's a silver lining. For one thing, it's easier to loosen up and take a full swing without the usual aches and pains. And that's great if you're one of those guys who thrive under those conditions. But if not, even then there's a bright side: you can blame the weather if you're not playing well. So if you're sweating buckets and can barely hold onto the club, set up your excuse for later by starting to grump about the humidity. Repeatedly wipe your brow and snap the sweat off your fingers, then be sure to let everyone notice that you're changing your golf glove. And if you get desperate, consider letting the club slide out of your hands as you're finishing a swing. That's when you take out a handkerchief or use a towel to wipe your forehead and say, "Man, this is brutal. The air's thick as soup out here. Way too humid to play well."

## "I thought all putts were supposed to break toward the water."

Ahh, putting. The bane of most golfers' existence. We all lose our touch from time to time, so in case you're going through a stretch where your hands are made of stone, it might be a good idea to suggest playing on a course with lots of water. You might have to donate a few balls to the drink, but there will surely be at least a few holes where there's a pond or a stream next to the green. So if by some remote chance you manage to hit an approach shot without getting wet and it actually lands somewhere in the vicinity of the pin, take a deep breath and let the pressure slide right off your shoulders. Even if your three-hundred-dollar putter lets you down, you're equipped with a built-in excuse. Your explanation when your ball turns north instead of south? Simple: "Omigosh! I swear that ball has a mind of its own! The brook was to my left, and the darned thing turned the other way. I thought all putts were supposed to break toward the water."

## *"It was too bright."*

Sometimes the prospect of a round of golf seems too good to be true. You're about to play with three of your good friends, it's a gorgeous day, the world is at peace, and your family and work situation couldn't be better. You can't wait to get to that first tee, it's great to be alive. Alas, despite the ideal circumstances, your "A game" is somewhere in outer space. But don't despair. That beautiful sunshine can come to your rescue. Dig your sunglasses out of your golf bag, put them on, take them off, and squint while mumbling about how the sun is hurting your eyes. Repeat a couple of times, and when the round is over, and the scorecard tells its sad story, you're prepared to explain why you weren't at your best. "Wow! How about that sun today! Couldn't even focus on the ball when I was setting up to swing. *Waaay* too bright!"

## *"I was trying to impress the cart boy/girl."*

It's automatic. When the beverage cart rolls around and the driver happens to be an attractive employee, sales and tips will go through the roof. Plus, it's a lock that someone in your foursome will make a pathetic attempt at flirting with them (usually the player whose belt has disappeared under their belly). But even if you're in great shape and have six-pack abs, this scenario can provide a plausible excuse when your game goes sour. Let's say it's one of those days. Nothing goes right, and you can feel it in your bones that there's no hope you're going to recover before the round is over. Take advantage of the opportunity by ordering more than you need from the cart worker, and pay them a compliment within earshot of everyone in your group. Then be sure to step up to your ball before they drive off. You're going to flub the shot anyway, and when you do, you will have established your excuse. "Did you see that beverage cart driver? I was so distracted, I just knew I would miss that shot."

### Did You Know?

*If you walk an average 18-hole course, you will travel approximately four miles and burn around 2,000 calories. Furthermore, according to the website ShapeFit.com, an average 190-pound golfer will burn approximately 431 calories per hour while walking the course. But if you ride in a cart, don't despair—you'll still burn roughly 1,300 calories over 18 holes.*

### "I thought trees were supposed to be 90 percent air."

There are times, although few and far between, that everything seems to go right on the course. You're on fire with pinpoint accuracy. But if you're anything like me, this is a rarity to say the least. Most days I'm all over the course and have to scramble to try and save par. So the next time you find yourself behind a tree, let your friends know that you see a way to save the hole. Sure, it's a difficult shot. Thankfully, you're an exceptional player. Then, when you hit the ball right into a branch, just retort with, "I thought trees were supposed to be 90 percent air; what gives?"

### "That was supposed to have been a practice swing."

Remember that Boy Scout motto: be prepared (of course, you're anything but a boy scout with all that malarkey about honesty and integrity and doing the right thing). No way. Otherwise, how can you come up with some underhanded strategy to explain a bad shot? So here's one to keep in your bag of tricks: Get in the habit of taking exactly four practice swings before every shot. Four swings. Not two or three.

Four! And take your time about it. Be so deliberate that you annoy your playing partners. That way they won't forget it if you need to spring this one on them later in the round. Let's say you're in a good position to make an approach shot, but you get a stab of doubt while you're standing over the ball. No matter how many times you try to set up, you can't shake the feeling that you're going to flub the shot. By no means should you go through with your usual routine. Take only three practice swings this time, so that if you do hit a bad shot, you have the perfect out, as follows: "Mulligan! Mulligan! That was supposed to be a practice swing! You guys know I take four swings every time before I actually mean to hit the ball!"

### *"I really need to stop going right for the pin."*

Sometimes the opportunity presents itself on the golf course to go for a birdie, but more often you need to control your wild side and play it safe to avoid a blowup hole. (*Hate* those triples and snowmen!) So if you find yourself in a funk, tell your playing partners that you're really juiced up today. You feel like being extra aggressive. Then, when your ball keeps finding the greenside bunkers, perhaps they'll buy the explanation of, "I've got to stop being so bold. I've been going right for the pin all day, and it's costing me dearly."

## *"I played with poor golfers, and they brought me down to their level."*

Let's say you've done some fast talking to get your spouse to agree that you can play golf on a Saturday while they stay at home with the kids. They're not happy, but when they reluctantly agree, you assure your better half that you're going to win the match and come home with a fistful of dollars. But alas, the golfing gods don't see it that way. It doesn't take long to realize that you have underestimated your opponents and overestimated yourself. So how are you going to get out of this situation and save face? First, offer up a silent thankyou to the inventors of the cell phone, and then call your spouse. Tell them that you were thinking of him/her and that you're looking forward to using part of your winnings to take them out to dinner. Of course you lose and come home with an empty wallet, but you're armed with a credible explanation. "Honey, believe me, I'm a much better golfer than those guys. I was way ahead when I called you, but they played so badly that they brought me down to their level and I ended up barely losing." And don't leave it at that. Back it up by pulling a pathetic face and say, "You know what? I hate to disappoint you, but this has left me with a headache and a terrible mood. If you don't mind, how about staying at home tonight and ordering a pizza?"

### *"I never play well on courses this hilly."*

You're playing on a mountain course that doesn't have even one flat hole. The tees are either elevated, or you're staring at a mountain when you have a driver in your hand. On top of that, your playing partners are a bunch of macho he-men who insist of carrying their bags so you're trudging like a mountaineer over hill and dale. But what they don't know is that this is a cake walk for you because you grew up in hill country, and you feel right at home in this environment. You're smiling to yourself because the other guys are already huffing and puffing and you have so much aerobic reserve that your confidence is higher than the surrounding moun-taintops. Still, you keep this information to yourself because, well, ya never know. And sure enough, even though you feel great physically, somehow your swing has abandoned you. Now's the time to say you need a break, like "Guys, let's slow down a bit. I can't catch my breath." And if you never find your swing, keep up the ruse. "Phew! I thought we were

supposed to be having fun. This is more like work!" And when all's said and done, and you're on the wrong end of the scorecard, no need to be humble or classy, especially since they don't know your history. This is the time to play your hole card. "Next time let's go back to a flat track. I'm not used to this elevation, so I never play well on courses this hilly."

### *"That bunker was in my blind spot."*

This is another one where you'll have to plant a seed some-where in the early or middle part of the round. Let's say you don't feel confident while standing over the ball, and you sense it's just a matter of time before you blow an important shot. You can't simply admit you choke at crucial moments, so what to do? There are as many answers as you have body parts. In this case, I would recommend blaming your spotty eyesight. Assuming you wear glasses, or at least carry a pair of shades, take them off at around hole ten, wipe them off, and study them as though there seems to be something wrong. Put them back on and take them off again, rub your eyes, and mumble just loudly enough so that your opponents can hear you say something about having blurry vision. And don't rely on this incident alone. Repeat your charade after another couple of holes, so when the match is tight, you will have done your homework. Eventually, the big test arrives. You have an easy approach shot, about 100 yards to the green. You take out your pitching wedge and again feel that stab of self-doubt. The pin is nestled tight against the right edge, so you play it safe by aiming for the middle, but sure enough, you blow the shot and push it to the right, directly into a steep bunker that's notorious for its difficulty. Of course, it takes you a few clumsy attempts to get out, but no problem. Simply look at your glasses again and say, "My eyes just aren't right today. That bunker must have been in my blind spot."

### *"I thought that putt was going to be a gimme."*

This round is for your foursome's summer championship. You've all been scoring close to your handicap and it's likely to be a tight match, so you want to have something in reserve as you get to the last couple of holes. This is the time to put on a show and appear to be magnanimous. When your opponents have a short putt that they're sure to make, pick it up for them and set a pattern by saying "You're good." And keep it up during the entire round, even though it's obvious, like when they leave one on the lip of the cup. Again, pick it up for them, and again say "You're good." The guy might look at you strangely, but you're planting the seed. So now, as anticipated, the match has gone back and forth and you're on the 18th green. Victory is yours if you can make a simple two-putt from 15 feet, but you get a case of the yips and leave it four feet short. Don't hesitate, just walk up to the ball with total confidence and pick it up. No doubt your opponents will insist you replace the ball and putt it, but you have done your homework. "What? No way! After all those putts I gave you today? C'mon now, I thought for sure that putt would be a gimme!"

## *"I was much better when I was younger."*

One of the great things about golf is that it's a lifetime sport. You can enjoy it from nine to ninety. But it's also true when they say, "Father Time is undefeated." So if the course is beating you like you've stolen its significant other, begin by slowly bending down to pick up your tee. Then, complain about how much your back and knees are bothering you. And of course, make sure to wax on poetically about the glory of your youth and how you long for the carefree days of yesteryear. And when you don't break 100, just tell your group, "Oh, when I was younger I used to be a scratch golfer."

## *"These shafts are too whippy for me."*

As we are all too well aware, golf is a difficult game at best. And it's such a mystery as to why. I mean, the ball isn't even moving! But alas, if you're having one of those days where nothing is going right, make sure to let your fellow golfers know that you're trying out a new set of clubs from the pro shop. After each errant shot, pick up the offensive club and examine it from head to toe. You might even want to pretend to check the flexibility of the weapon. Then, when the round mercifully comes to an end, make sure to state in your most authoritative voice, "I've never played golf with shafts that were so whippy. No wonder I played so poorly."

## *"I skipped church this morning, and now God is getting even with me."*

C'mon, now. You haven't been to church for three years, but what the heck. When it comes to salvation you're already on the wrong list, so why not tell a little white lie and invoke God to get you off the hook when you screw up on the golf course? As they say, if you're in for an inch, you're in for a mile. So there's your answer. If you've played like you've never had a golf club in your hand before, put a guilty look on your face, hang your head like a choir boy, and say, "Because this round was scheduled so early, I didn't have time to go to church today." Then, if things don't improve by the end of the round, hit 'em with, "I knew I shouldn't have skipped church this morning. Now God's getting even with me. Next week I'll have to put some hard cash in the collection plate." Just make sure not to stand in a puddle if there's a lightning storm anywhere within ten miles. God's funny that way.

> ## Did You Know?
> The world's longest golf hole is the mammoth 909-yard 7th hole at the Satsuki Golf Club in Japan.

### "The lip of the hole was pushed up, and my ball rimmed out."

I know, I know, you are a terrific putter. In reality you have the hand of a neurosurgeon. But even the best putters can have an off day. On that rare occasion that your putter seems to have failed you, start to complain about the quality of the greens. The holes for the pins seem to have been installed by four-year-olds. Then, when you miss your next easy putt, retort with, "That ball would have gone straight in if the lip of the hole weren't askew. The grounds crew really should be fired."

### *"I'm much better on the longer putts."*

You are in a cart vs. cart contest, and the match has been neck and neck the entire round. Your putter has been on fire, cozying up to your long putts for gimmes on almost every hole and taunting your opponents by obnoxiously celebrating and high-fiving your partner. The match is even going into the 18th, and you're the only one who reaches the green in regulation. Your partner is already out of it, and both of your opponents chip on and end up with tap-in bogeys. Now it's a simple matter for you to two-putt and win the match. As usual, you put a nice smooth stroke on your first putt and end up just short, three feet below the pin. You anticipate another gimme from your opponents, but it's a money match and they aren't about to give it to you. No biggee, you step up and prepare to deliver the coup de grâce, but just in case you get a case of the yips you plan ahead and let everyone know how much better you are on the longer putts. And lo and behold, you miss the three-footer. This leads to a putting contest on the practice green to determine the match, and once more you miss a short putt and give your opponents an early Christmas present. No problem. You're not about to take the high road and apologize. "Hey there, partner, what can I tell you? I'm way better on the long putts, and I can't believe those guys didn't concede that gimme on the 18th."

### *"I had the worst night's sleep."*

I hope you understand that this one applies even if you slept like a log and woke up singing "Oh, what a beautiful morning" at the top of your lungs. Not only that, it'll work regardless of your demeanor at the beginning of the round. Throw caution to the winds. Talk some trash. Strut around like you're king of the world. Remind your opponents about the time you won by a dozen strokes. Then, when your performance becomes as sad as a dog who's pooped on the living room rug, that's when you pull out your acting skills. Produce a long, audible yawn and then pretend to nod off in the cart. When you're about to putt, step away, rub your eyes, and shake your head like you're trying to clear the cobwebs. And if no one seems to notice, slap your own face as loudly as you can, yell "C'mon, wake up!", and then repeat the previous performance while you have their attention. From then on you have nothing to lose. Maybe your game will come around. Great, collect your winnings and taunt your opponents by bragging that you kicked their butts even though you were only half awake. But if you lose, it's a no-brainer. Repeat after me: "Jeez, if you guys had any class you wouldn't even accept my money. I never had a worse night's sleep. How could I score when I couldn't keep my eyes open?"

## *"I forgot my hat."*

It's generally useful to blame some piece of equipment for a bad round, like "These grips are all wrong," "I usually play with a different ball," or "I'm still not used to these clubs." But if you're playing with your usual weekend foursome, and they know that you're using exactly the same equipment that you've had for the past two years, you'll need to get a bit more creative. How about complaining that you forgot your hat? "But what if I was wearing a hat?", you might ask. No problem. Just wait until you come to the next men's room, then while you're in there, take off your hat and stuff it in your pocket until you can sneak it in your bag. After a hole or two, one of your playing partners might notice that you're not wearing it. That's when you slap your thigh and say, "Damn! I must have left it in the men's room!" Then, when the round is over and as usual you are on the wrong end of the scorecard, your devious preparation will have paid off. "Can you believe it? I forgot my hat in that men's room and it threw off my entire game."

### *"I overslept and didn't have time to get to the range before the round."*

On any given day, if it becomes obvious after a few holes that you've left your swing in your car and your putter feels like a wet noodle in your hands, don't say anything at first but begin to do a lot of practice swings as though you're trying to find your groove. Carry on every time you flub a shot, maybe curse a bit and even throw a club or two. Then start to complain under your breath (but loud enough to be heard) about how unreliable your alarm clock is. Then, when you've gone down to ignominious defeat, put on a classy act by apologizing to your partners. "Sorry guys, I hope I didn't spoil the round for you. I overslept this morning and didn't get a chance to get on the practice range before we came out here."

### *"I don't like teeing off last all of the time."*

Sure, you love the game of golf. And it doesn't matter that you're a terrible golfer. If you can just muster up one or two decent shots a round, that is enough to keep you coming back. Unfortunately, your game is so pathetic that you rarely tee off first. After losing hole after hole, you are relegated to your spot at the back of the line. If this sounds like you, let your compatriots know that you've completely lost your confidence. And if they offer to let you tee off first, just politely decline, stating that you respect the etiquette of the game too much to break the rules. But when the round is over, try this excuse on for size: "If I could only win a couple of holes and tee off first, I'm sure my confidence and game would improve."

### *"I can't play with plastic spikes in my golf shoes."*

Many courses now prohibit playing with metal golf spikes due to the damage they can cause to the greens. So why not use this to your advantage? When you're having one of those days where nothing seems to be going right, make sure to take a big swing right where everyone can see you. Then, make sure to take a stumble. Or, if you really want to lay it on thick, fall flat on your back. And definitely don't forget to yell out in frustration, "I just can't keep my feet under me with these pathetic plastic spikes."

### *"My hat is too tight, and it's cutting off circulation to my brain."*

The following excuse is one of the lamest ones ever, but if you can't come up with anything else, well, desperate times, desperate measures . . . Suppose you've been playing lights out and you shoot your best score ever on the front nine. You're strutting around like a rooster and counting your winnings as you make the turn, but as they say, "pride goeth before the fall." Your tee shot on hole ten goes out of bounds, you have to tee it up again, and this time you're behind a tree. By the time this nightmare ends you've racked up a "snowman" quadruple bogey and it gets worse from there. After two more disastrous holes there's no chance to recover. You haven't complained about anything up 'til now, so where are you going to place the blame on this pathetic collapse? No problem. Start to fidget with your hat. Loosen the clasp in the back, and then loosen it again. Rub your temples as though your head's killing you, then look at the hat again as if you can't figure out what's wrong with it. And when you finish the round, "discover" what the problem has been. "Oh my God! This thing's a size 7 and ⅛ and I wear a 7 and ¾!" Then quickly put the hat in your bag so no one can look at it, and smack your leg in frustration. "No wonder I couldn't concentrate on the back nine. This thing's been cutting off the circulation to my brain!"

## "The GPS on this cart is clearly wrong."

There's a story about Ben Hogan when he asked his caddy the distance to the pin. As the story goes, the caddy consulted his notes and said, "It's between 146 and 147 yards." To which Hogan replied, "Well, which one is it?" No need for the caddy's advice on distance these days because GPS devices give you that information instantaneously. Now all you have to do is choose the right club, make the right swing, and enjoy watching the ball land on the green and cozy up to the hole. But let's say you get the yardage, take your shot, and land a good thirty or more yards short of the green. There's money on the line, and you don't want to look like an idiot in front of your playing partner, so you have to think fast. Make a show of using the GPS again, and then put it down in disgust while saying, "I just put the perfect six-iron on that ball, and there's no way it should have landed that short. There's gotta be something wrong with this GPS!"

### *"I've been at it for years and still have absolutely no idea how to play this crazy sport!"*

This is the excuse of all excuses, the one to use when all else fails and you can't get off the tee or out of the trap. Your iron game has completely fallen apart, and you're ecstatic with a three putt. When you have so many snowmen on your card that it looks like the North Pole. You've used every excuse in this book on multiple occasions, and you are contemplating giving up this great game of golf for Lent. Take a deep breath, remember that hitting a good golf shot, no matter how infrequent, is a high like no other, and then scream from the mountain tops those immortal words that have been said by every man, woman, or child to ever play the great game of golf: "I have absolutely no idea what the hell I'm doing! What time do we tee off tomorrow?"

## Did You Know?

*John Anthony Hudson is believed to be the only person to card holes in one at consecutive holes at a major golf tournament. Hudson pulled off the unlikely feat by acing the 195-yard 11th hole with a 4-iron, and then the 311-yard par 4 12th by using his driver at the second round of the 1971 Martini International Tournament.*